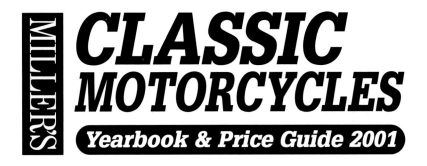

MILLER'S
CLASSIC
MOTORCYCLES
Yearbook & Price Guide 2001

MILLER'S CLASSIC MOTORCYCLES YEARBOOK AND PRICE GUIDE 2001

Created and designed by
Miller's Publications
The Cellars, High Street
Tenterden, Kent TN30 6BN
Telephone: 01580 766411
Fax: 01580 766100

General Editor: Mick Walker
Editorial and Production Co-ordinator: Ian Penberthy
Editorial Assistants: Rosemary Cooke, Carol Gillings, Lalage Johnstone
Designers: Philip Hannath, Kari Reeves
Advertisement Designer: Simon Cook
Advertising Executive: Jo Hill
Advertising Assistant: Melinda Williams
Production Assistants: Elaine Burrell, Gillian Charles
Additional Photography: Ian Booth, David Hawtin,
David Merewether, Robin Saker
Indexer: Hilary Bird

First published in Great Britain in 2000
by Miller's, a division of Mitchell Beazley,
imprints of Octopus Publishing Group Ltd,
2–4 Heron Quays, London E14 4JP

© 2000 Octopus Publishing Group Ltd

A CIP catalogue record for this book is
available from the British Library

ISBN 1 84000 312 X

Black and white Illustrations and film output by CK Litho, Whitstable, Kent
Colour origination by Pica Colour Separation Overseas Pte Ltd, Singapore
Printed and bound by Toppan Printing Co (HK) Ltd, China

Front cover illustration:

1969 BSA Rocket 3. **£4,500–5,000 PC**

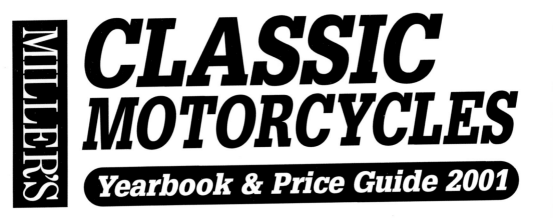

MILLER'S

CLASSIC MOTORCYCLES

Yearbook & Price Guide 2001

General Editor
Mick Walker

Foreword by
Arthur Wheeler

Contents

Acknowledgements

The publishers would like to acknowledge the great assistance given by our consultants:

Malcolm Barber	81 Westside, London SW4 9AY Tel: 0171 228 8000
Rob Carrick	5 Tinkers Lane, Wimbotsham, King's Lynn, Norfolk PE34 3QE Tel: 01366 388801
David Hawkins	81 Westside, London SW4 9AY Tel: 0171 228 8000
Michael Jackson	Sotheby's, 34–35 New Bond Street, London SW1A 2AA Tel: 0171 493 8080
Brian Verrall	Caffyns Row, High Street, Handcross, Nr Haywards Heath, West Sussex RH17 6BJ Tel: 01444 400678
Rick Walker	R&M Walker, 45 Caves Close, Terrington St Clement, King's Lynn, Norfolk Tel: 01553 829141

We would like to extend our thanks to all auction houses, their press offices, and dealers who have assisted us in the production of this book, along with the organisers and press offices of the following events:

The International Classic Bike Show
Louis Vuitton Classic

Foreword

I was pleased to be asked to write this Foreword for the 2001 edition of *Miller's Classic Motorcycle Yearbook & Price Guide* by my old friend and fellow racer Mick Walker. Browsing through its pages brought back so many memories of the machines I had encountered during my long racing career.

I feel extremely fortunate to have lived a life full of excitement and to have raced during what is now regarded as the classic era – the golden years – of motorcycle sport.

I grew up with motorcycles, as my uncle, Frank Taylor, was a road racer during the 1920s, and I was always hanging around his workshop. When I was 12, I exchanged some old radio parts for a Scott, which I used to ride around my grandfather's yard. I bought my first road bike when I was 17, but soon sold it to buy a Big Port AJS grasstrack machine and entered my first race at Leatherhead in 1934. Although I continued to ride in grasstrack events until 1948, I had raced a borrowed 500 clubman's machine at Brooklands in 1936 and began riding my own Mk V KTT Velocette in 1937 at Brooklands and the Manx Grand Prix at the Isle of Man shortly after. Eventually I switched to road racing exclusively and have ridden a variety of classic machines in competition, including Moto Guzzi 250 and 350, FB Mondial 125, MV 125, Ducati 125, AJS and Matchless.

I retired from racing in 1962, finishing third in the 250cc World Championship that year. Then I was invited to ride in demo laps at the Isle of Man and various other circuits toward the end of the 1970s, and I thought to myself, 'This is pretty good.' Thus I made my 'comeback' in classic racing during the 1980s and have been active in the sport ever since. Today, I ride in historic racing events throughout Europe, and even New Zealand. It's wonderful to see and hear those classic machines on the track again, doing what they were designed to do, rather than gathering dust in some forgotten corner.

I do hope you will find *Miller's Classic Motorcycle Yearbook & Price Guide 2001* as fascinating as I do. Not only does it provide an intriguing glimpse of the history of motorcycling on road and track, but it also offers the enthusiast and collector a treasure trove of information that will prove invaluable when sourcing and buying the classic machine of your dreams.

Arthur Wheeler

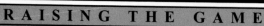

Maintaining Classic Bike Engines

A well-serviced bike is a treat to ride. Knowing that it will fire up easily and pull away without fuss takes a lot of stress out of owning a classic bike. It can also pay dividends when it comes to selling the machine – knowing that it will start without any problems, tick over without any undue clanks and rattles, and not pollute the atmosphere with noxious exhaust emissions.

The regular maintenance of a classic bike engine can be split into two distinct aspects: first, a general visual inspection should be carried out every time the bike is used; secondly, a more intricate check, when various covers have to be removed for an in-depth inspection, should be carried out on a calendar or mileage basis.

Understanding what is required by way of preventative maintenance will pay dividends in extended engine life and reduced repair bills. The entire subject of engine maintenance would fill the pages of a decent-sized manual, but only the areas that concern the DIY biker – with limited ability – will be dealt with here. An owner who wishes to service his or her machine should have a modestly equipped workshop, a set of correctly-sized spanners and a workshop manual that covers the bike in question.

As a motorcycle user, it is not enough simply to be able to ride a machine, for some form of mechanical knowledge is essential to prevent overstressing or under-maintaining the working parts of the engine. Many classic bikes in use today were rebuilt by their owners, who know their internal workings intimately. But there are countless newcomers to the world of classic motorcycling who have never seen inside the engines of their bikes.

Carrying out routine maintenance tasks need not be a chore and can be very therapeutic. It can save you money, too, provided the work is carried out 'to the book'. The local bike dealer's servicing bills will be eliminated and any lurking fault can be nipped in the bud before a major disaster occurs. Most scheduled jobs do not take much time at all, but a dedicated owner can make them last for hours if need be!

First-line – or daily – servicing should include a good inspection of the engine, its mountings, cables and pipework to ensure that all items are secure. All nuts, bolts and connections must be tight, while locking devices (lock wire, lock washers, split pins, etc) must be intact. Oil leaks should be looked for at this stage, too.

The main point of this primary inspection is to ensure that all fluid levels are correct, and that enough lubricant is available for the forthcoming ride. With a classic machine that has been idle for some time, a degree of 'wet sumping' will occur – that is oil will tend to collect in the bottom of the crankcase. To check the oil level in the tank, first run the engine off load to return the contents of the sump to the oil tank. The amount may range from a spoonful to a couple of pints, depending on the period of idleness and the oil pump condition. Many an unwary owner has topped up the tank before starting the engine, and ended up with an extra couple of pints on the garage floor.

Second-line servicing is more involved. It includes oil and filter changes, and making checks on tappet clearance, ignition timing, spark plug condition and gap, and carburettor settings. As each motorcycle will require a different method of completing these checks, it is best to refer to the relevant manual and follow it to the letter. Many checks should be carried out at specific mileages, but owning a classic bike is not about covering vast commuter distances, so a logical schedule should be worked out and adhered to. For example, Norton originally specified that the engine oil in its twin-cylinder models should be changed every 2,000 miles. As classics, the same machines are subjected to shorter, less frequent outings, so this distance should be halved, and if the annual mileage is below that figure, change the oil every year prior to the winter lay-up. The reason for changing the oil before the winter lull is to protect against internal corrosion. On short journeys, the acids of combustion are not boiled off and circulate with the lubricant. If these acids are allowed to remain in the engine over the winter, they will begin to eat away at the bearing surfaces. The best plan is to fill the engine with a cheap oil for the lay-up, and change it for a better grade during the spring, before the forthcoming riding season. Many other servicing tasks are called for at greater mileages, but it is prudent to carry them out during the spring inspection.

The classic scene today is one of a happy band of enthusiasts who like to ride and are willing to help other owners in trouble. There are many regional one-make clubs and just as many local groups of national clubs, whose membership includes some very knowledgeable riders with years of experience. The magazines published by national clubs also offer hints and tips on owning and servicing classic machines.

Operating a classic motorcycle does not mean having to spend countless hours in the shed on tedious rectification jobs, for with modern equipment, uprated electrics and electronic ignition systems, and most of all modern high-quality oils, the classic bike has become a reliable machine that can be ridden with pride.

Happy riding.

Rob Carrick

The Motorcycle Market

The past 12 months have seen some exciting and some sad developments in the motorcycle auction market, which has probably been as buoyant as it was in the heady late 1980s, some prices equalling and even exceeding the highest achieved in those days. A strong pound does not appear to have discouraged overseas buyers, and this, in turn, has ensured a strong defensive home market, too. Sotheby's held only two UK sales that included motorcycles, in April and July 1999, both with mixed success, although a nice original 1915 New Hudson in 'as found' condition managed £3,105 and a 1947 Manx Norton Model 40 brought £4,370.

A 1913 Scott, with excellent provenance and high rarity value, astonished everyone by making a resounding £18,400. However, it was the only exceptional UK motorcycle price achieved by Sotheby's, and toward the end of 1999 the company announced that it was closing its UK motor department.

Sotheby's held a motorcycle and bicycle only sale in Chicago in September 1999, at which some excellent prices were realised for American machines, but this would appear to be its sole remaining annual motorcycle sale. Highlights in Chicago included a stunning 1939 Indian Four at $60,950, a 1948 Indian Chief at $41,400 and a rare 1906 Indian at $25,300, with a 1938 'Knuckle-head' Harley-Davidson making $26,459. Sotheby's is not withdrawing from the market completely, having formed a partnership with Poulain Le Fur in Paris. So far, however, no motorcycles have been offered.

A newcomer to the motorcycle auction world, in the shape of H & H in Buxton, held its first all-bike sale last September, raising £200,000. Just under 50 per cent of machines consigned were sold, the highest price being £16,125, paid for a 1955 Vincent Black Prince. This was closely followed by a 1931 Harley-Davidson, at £10,750, and another Vincent, a 1952 Rapide, which made £12,362. H & H's March 2000 sale was smaller, totalling £96,514. The highest price was the £11,287 paid for a 1920 Norton 490cc Brooklands Special.

For many years, Palmer Snell has been the only provincial auction house to hold regular motorcycle sales, and it was back at The Royal Bath & West Showground at Shepton Mallet in October. With 71 catalogued entries, the sale was smaller than previous events, and taking into account some late entries, about 50 per cent found buyers, Palmer Snell concentrating on 'bread-and-butter' bikes rather than exotics. The company's March 2000 sale was a modest event with 39 entries.

Coy's and BCA occasionally include single machines in their car sales, but do not seriously pursue the two-wheeled market. However, another new entry into the ranks is Cheffins Grain and Comins in Cambridgeshire. Under the direction of Julian Schoolheifer, its sale in April included 11 bikes, of which eight sold, which is a promising start.

It has to be said that Brooks continues to dominate the motorcycle auction market, and with sales held at Stafford in April and October, the National Motor Museum, Beaulieu (a more recent venue for bikes) in July and September, Harrogate and Olympia, London, in December 1999, it is hardly surprising that motorcycle sales topped £2 million in that year. The figure pales, however, when compared with the result from The International Classic Motorcycle Show at Stafford in April 2000, which totalled £1.15 million, a record for a motorcycle auction held anywhere.

The oft-repeated truisms that top bikes make top money and that single-owner collections command a premium over multi-consignment sales were emphasised again and again, and Brooks did particularly well with Brough-Superiors. At Stafford in April 1999, a 1937 990cc SS100 model sold for £39,100, while a 1925 SS80 achieved £13,800. At Beaulieu in July 1999, a 1931 SS100 soared to make £32,488 and a 1929 SS80 brought £11,615, a 1913 W. E. Brough (made by George Brough's father) also doing well at £11,500.

The same sale at Beaulieu saw a 1924 NUT 700cc V-twin change hands for £11,500 and a 1914 Matchless 990cc Model H fetch £10,810, while a 1954 Norton Manx made £10,063, a 1915 Indian £9,200, and a 1909 Premier V-twin £8,970. At the *Classic Mechanics* Show at Stafford in October 1999, a 1954 Vincent Black Shadow with Steib sidecar made £16,963 and another Brough, a 1937 SS80, took £15,180.

New records were broken at Stafford in April 2000, when a 1954 AJS Porcupine E95 racer, from the Arter collection, sold for £157,700 (an auction record for a British machine) and a spare E95 engine went to an American buyer for £78,500 – the highest price paid for an engine at auction. A 1955 Matchless G45 racer brought £20,125, reflecting its documented racing provenance, and another Brough-Superior, a 1936 SS100, went to a French buyer for £42,200 – a price equal to the highest previously achieved for this model in October 1989.

That some of the highest prices at this sale were paid by overseas enthusiasts indicates that the strength of sterling is no deterrent when quality is on offer, and the record sale total was gratifying also for Morton's Motorcycle Media, the new owners of The International Classic Motorcycle Show at Stafford, who worked with Alan Whitehead as consultant and guiding hand. The Show enjoyed a record turn-out in terms of public attendance and numbers of stalls booked, and with such a heartening result for the first major sale of the year, I have every confidence in a buoyant market for the coming 12 months.

Malcolm Barber

Aermacchi *(Italian 1950–78)*

◄ **1965 Aermacchi Ala Verde,** 248cc, overhead-valve single, 5-speed gearbox, Borrani alloy rims, otherwise largely standard.
£1,400–1,600 H&H

The Ala Verde had an engine and frame that were very similar to the company's racing machines.

AJS *(British 1909–66)*

◄ **1922 AJS V-twin,** 799cc, side-valve engine, single carburettor, footboards, unrestored.
£4,250–4,750 YEST

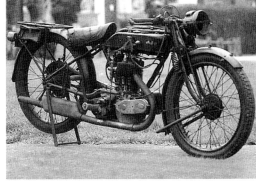

1922 AJS Model B1, 349cc, in need of restoration.
£2,450–2,700 BKS

When AJS produced this machine, the company was riding on the crest of a wave. It employed approximately 600 people and was basking in the glory of a TT double achieved by Eric Williams in the Junior and Harold R. Davies in the Senior. The victory in the Senior was made all the more glorious because a 350-class machine had achieved it. The company sought to capitalise on its success by introducing two new models in 1922, aimed at those seeking sporting mounts. Both were 2¾hp machines with three-speed gearboxes derived from the Model B touring. The B1 was offered with TT-pattern handlebars and footrests instead of footboards, while the B2 came in stripped form without a kickstart and with lighter tinware.

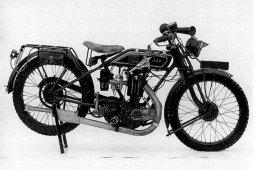

1923 AJS Big Port, 349cc, in need of restoration.
£3,600–4,000 TEN

The legendary Big Port model was introduced at the 1922 Olympia Motor Cycle Show in London. The series was noted for the size of its exhaust valve – considerably larger than competitors' models.

► **1926 AJS Big Port Model G6,** 349cc, overhead-valve single.
£6,500–7,200 BKS

AJS offered three Big Port models for 1926: the GR7 racer, the G7 Special Sports and the G6 touring model. The last weighed about 218lb compared to the GR7, which tipped the scales at 203lb and utilised plain bushes instead of the roller- and ball-bearings found on the other two for the timing gears and mainshafts. A Lucas magneto provided ignition in all cases, while the final drive was transmitted through a three-speed gearbox.

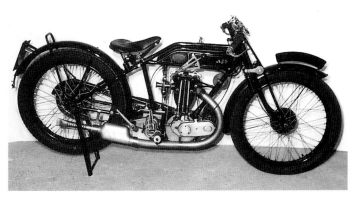

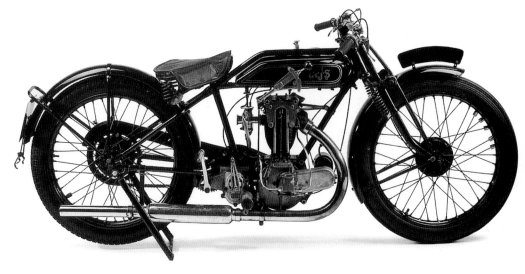

1927 AJS H6 Big Port, 349cc, overhead-valve single, girder forks, rigid frame, restored, very good condition.
£5,500–6,000 S

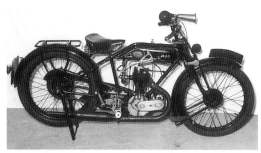

1927 AJS Model H4, 349cc, side-valve single,
Binks carburettor, Lucas magneto, 3-speed
countershaft gearbox.
£4,900–5,400 BKS

The AJS range for 1927 included four 348cc singles,
three of which had side-valve engines. The cheapest
was the H5 Standard Sporting model, listed at
£44.0s.0d. This was complemented by two De Luxe
models, the H3 Touring and the H4 Sporting,
both priced at £48.10s.0d. The two De Luxe models
had fittings appropriate to their intended role,
the H4 having footrests and sporting handlebars.

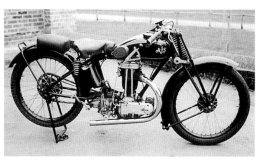

1931 AJS SB6 Big Port, 348cc, overhead-valve single,
74 x 81mm bore and stroke.
£2,650–3,000 BKS

The SB6 was the first machine to leave the AJS
factory officially bearing the Big Port name.
Essentially, it was a single-port version of the
twin-port S6, designed to take advantage of the
concessionary tax rate for machines weighing less
than 224lb and, as such, came equipped with a
three-speed Sturmey Archer gearbox. A four-speed
gearbox was available as an option, although this
raised the weight above the favourable limit.
To keep the weight down to the required level,
no front stand or rear carrier were fitted.

1929 AJS Model 9, 499cc, side-valve single,
84 x 90mm bore and stroke.
£2,700–3,000 BLM

The Model 9 series continued until the late 1930s,
but from the beginning of the 1930s, the cylinder
was inclined some 10 degrees from the vertical.

1930 AJS Big Port, 349cc, late model with round tank,
original specification.
£4,000–4,500 MAY

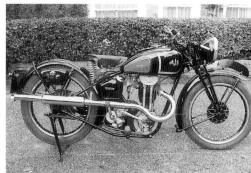

1937 AJS Model 22, 245cc, overhead-valve single,
62.5 x 80mm bore and stroke, high-level exhaust.
£2,800–3,100 VER

1937 AJS Model 2, 982cc, side-valve V-twin, 85.5 x 85.5mm bore and stroke.
£6,400–7,100 **BKS**

The big AJS side-valve V-twin was the first model to display the influence of the firm's new owner, Matchless, when a revised version was released in 1932. The power unit was essentially the same as that found in the comparable Matchless. As with the Collier brothers' product, the big twin found favour with sidecar exponents, as well as riders who appreciated the machine's ability to offer high-speed touring in a relaxed manner. During 1933, an export variant was added with a foot-operated clutch, swept-back handlebars and the gear lever on the left-hand side of the fuel tank.

1938 AJS Model 22, 245cc, overhead-valve, twin-port single, original and unrestored.
£3,500–4,000 **AMOC**

1950 AJS Model 18S, 497cc, overhead-valve single, 82.5 x 93mm bore and stroke, swinging-arm rear suspension with 'candlestick' suspension units, original condition.
£2,100–2,400 **TEN**

The Model 18S entered production in 1949.

◀ **1959 AJS Model 16MS,** 348cc, overhead-valve single, 69 x 93mm bore and stroke.
£1,800–2,000 **BLM**

This late AMC big single employed the same cycle parts as the Model 18.

1963 AJS Model 18S, 497cc, overhead-valve, pre-unit single, 4-speed gearbox, full-width alloy hubs.
£2,000–2,300 **PBM**

During 1962 and 1963, the Model 18 was also known as the Statesman – the prefix 'Elder' should have been added, given its length of service. After the 1963 model year, the 18 was given a shorter-stroke engine.

1959 AJS Model 31, 646cc, overhead-valve twin, 72 x 79.3mm bore and stroke.
£2,400–2,700 **BLM**

The Model 31's first year of production was 1959.

Alldays *(British 1915–20s)*

◀ **1920 Alldays Allon,** 292cc, 2-stroke single.
£2,000–2,250 BKS

The Birmingham based company Alldays
Allon began building motorcycles in
1915 and ceased during the 1920s.
Today, these machines are very rare, but
because of their humble, basic-transport
roots – and the use of a two-stroke engine –
they can't be considered classics.

Ariel *(British 1902–70)*

1926 Ariel Model A, 497cc, side-valve single.
£3,000–3,500 AOC/AOM

1939 Ariel Red Hunter, 349cc, overhead-valve single,
plunger rear suspension, girder forks.
£1,800–2,200 AT

1949 Ariel Red Hunter, 349cc, overhead-valve single, 4-speed foot-change gearbox, telescopic forks, rigid frame,
concours condition.
£4,200–4,600 BKS

◀ **1949 Ariel KG 500,** 499cc, overhead-valve
twin, 63 x 80mm bore and stroke, 4-speed foot-
change gearbox, rigid frame, concours condition.
£2,800–3,100 BKS

The enthusiastic greeting that met the
release of the 500cc Triumph Speed Twin
compelled other British manufacturers to
develop similar machines. However, it was
not until peace returned after WWII that
new models began to emerge.
Ariel introduced its entry into the
increasingly competitive market in 1948.
The new twin was offered in two forms:
the de luxe KG and sporting KH Red Hunter.

⬦52 Ariel Square Four, 995cc, plunger rear suspension.
£,000–3,300 BRIT

⬦uring the late 1920s, the renowned designer Edward
⬦rner joined Ariel and promptly created the first of the
⬦quare Fours. A landmark design, initially it displaced
⬦8cc and had a chain-driven overhead camshaft.
⬦evised models of 600 and 998cc followed. A major
⬦design took place in 1952, with the adoption of an
⬦-alloy, overhead-valve engine with coil ignition.
⬦is later model was only produced in 995cc form.

⬦1955 Ariel NH, 346cc, overhead-valve single,
⬦2 x 85mm bore and stroke, standard specification.
⬦,700–1,900 BKS

⬦or the 1954 season, Ariel introduced a new
⬦winging-arm frame, which was to be utilised on
⬦e majority of the company's singles and twins.

⬦956 Ariel LH Colt, 198cc, overhead-valve single,
⬦0 x 70mm bore and stroke, telescopic forks,
⬦unger rear suspension, dualseat.
⬦450–500 PM

⬦competitor of the Triumph Cub, the Colt shared
⬦any basic features with the BSA C10 and C11
⬦ngles. It was built between 1954 and 1959.

Cross Reference
See Colour Review

⬦956 Ariel FH Huntmaster, 647cc, overhead-valve twin,
⬦0 x 84mm bore and stroke, telescopic forks, swinging-
⬦rm rear suspension, full-width alloy drum brakes,
⬦eadlamp nacelle, standard specification.
⬦2,300–2,600 BLM

1953 Ariel KH, 499cc, overhead-valve, pre-unit twin,
63 x 80mm bore and stroke, 4-speed foot-change
gearbox, telescopic forks, rigid frame.
£2,200–2,500 AOC/AOM

Put into production in 1948, the KH followed a trend
pioneered by Edward Turner's mould-breaking
Triumph Speed Twin of 1938.

1958 Ariel VH Red Hunter, 499cc, overhead-valve single, telescopic forks, swinging-arm rear suspension, full-width hubs, headlamp nacelle.
£2,700–3,000 BLM

The 1958 model was the final version of the long-running Red Hunter series.

1958 Ariel FH Huntmaster, 646cc, overhead-valve twin.
£2,200–2,600 BLM

The Huntmaster was clearly based on the BSA A10 series, even sharing the same engine capacity.

1960 Ariel Arrow, 247cc, air-cooled, 2-stroke twin, standard specification.
£1,200–1,400 H&H

The Arrow was basically a naked Leader.

1964 Ariel Arrow 200, 199cc, 2-stroke twin, 48.5 x 54mm bore and stroke, restored to original specification.
£1,200–1,400 CGC

The rarest of all the twin-cylinder, two-stroke Ariels, the Arrow 200 was only built in 1964 and 1965, and numbers sold were small. The change in engine capacity was achieved by decreasing the bore size.

1958 Ariel Square Four 4G Mk 2, 995cc, overhead-valve four, alloy heads, full-width hubs, headlamp nacelle.
£4,100–4,600 AOC/AOM

The final variant of the Square Four retained plunger rear suspension.

1959 Ariel Leader, 247cc, air-cooled, 2-stroke twin, alloy heads, cast-iron cylinders.
£1,400–1,700 AT

Designed by Val Page and launched in 1958, the Leader broke with British tradition in its frame and suspension layout. It employed a stiff, fabricated steel beam, instead of tubes, and a trailing-link front fork.

1961 Ariel Arrow, 247cc, air-cooled, 2-stroke twin, fitted with Ace handlebars (as on sports Golden Arrow) and factory Avonaire fairing.
£1,400–1,600 BLM

1962 Ariel Arrow Sports, 247cc, air-cooled, 2-stroke twin, original, in need of restoration.
£500–550 BKS

Beardmore-Precision
(British 1906–23)

◄ **1923 Beardmore-Precision Model D,** 350cc, side-valve single, high-level exhaust.
£2,500–2,800 BKS

Frank Baker founded the F. E. Baker Company in 1906 and began making cycle fittings under the Precision trademark. It was not until 1910 that he entered motorcycle production, but at the 1911 Olympia show no fewer than 96 machines had Precision engines. In 1919, William Beardmore & Co had injected capital to create Beardmore-Precision. Despite this and the company's remarkable start, by 1924, sales were sliding dramatically and, in a last-ditch effort to boost interest, machines were prepared for that year's TT, but the attempt failed dismally. This caused Beardmore to withdraw support and the company was wound up.

Benelli *(Italian 1911–)*

Six *fratelli* (brothers) created a small workshop in the Adriatic coastal township of Pesaro; the year was 1911. From this humblest of beginnings would spring one of the most famous of all Italian marques. At first, the workshop's activities were restricted to the repair of automobiles and motorcycles, and anything else mechanical, even guns. But soon the brothers began to manufacture component parts, a process that accelerated with the outbreak of WWI in 1914.

At the end of hostilities in 1918, the brothers turned their attention to a new field – cheap commuter transport. Thus, the Benellis designed and built their first engine, a 98cc two-stroke. Unfortunately, the idea of fitting this unit to a conventional pedal cycle proved disastrous. Undaunted, they proceeded to design a complete motorcycle.

Launched in 1921, the new Benelli soon proved a sales success, helped by the track exploits of the youngest brother, Tonino, who began racing in 1923 at Monza. From then until 1932, Tonino Benelli scored victory after victory. Then he retired and became the factory's tester. And it was

on a testing sortie that this most daring of the Benelli brothers met his death in September 1937.

But the racing connection was continued, and Ted Mellors won the 1939 Lightweight TT in the Isle of Man on a 250 double-overhead-camshaft Benelli single.

As soon as WWII was over in 1945, Benelli re-established itself in racing, but withdrew from competition after its number-one rider, Dario Ambrosini, was killed while practising for the French Grand Prix in 1951.

The company returned to the fray in 1959 with an updated 250cc single, with Duke, Dale and Grassetti at the controls. But this attempt met with little success, so Benelli concentrated on developing a brand-new four-cylinder GP bike, and the effort was rewarded when Benelli won its second world title (Ambrosini had won its first in 1950) in 1969, with the Australian Kel Carruthers.

After De Tomaso took over the company in the early 1970s, Benelli built and marketed a series of Japanese-inspired, overhead-camshaft four- and six-cylinder models.

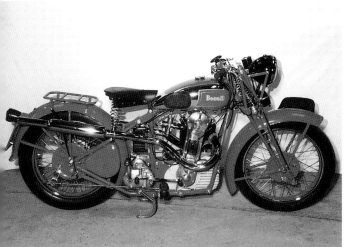

◄ **1938 Benelli Turismo 4TN,** 500cc, overhead-camshaft, twin-port single, 4-speed foot-change gearbox, completely restored to concours condition.
£6,300–7,000 BKS

The design features of Ted Mellors' 'double-knocker' 249cc unsupercharged Benelli, with which he beat the supercharged DKW to gain his first TT win, became commonplace in post-war lightweight Italian classics. An alloy, bolted-on cambox, with enclosed overhead camshafts operating exposed hairpin springs and driven by a long train of gears, was a feature used to great effect by MV Agusta in later years. This arrangement was also adopted by Benelli for a larger-capacity 500cc, overhead-camshaft single in 1935.

BMW *(German 1923–)*

One of the truly great names of both motorcycle and car worlds, BMW (*Bayerische Motoren Werke*) owes its existence to a merger, in 1913, between two aero-engine manufacturers. This resulted in the creation of BFW (*Bayerische Flugzeug Werke*) in 1916; BMW arrived in the following year.

Both BFW and BMW were major suppliers of engines to the German air force during WWI, and the two most important men in BMW's story at the time were an Italian-born Austrian banker, Camillo Castiglione, and a youthful Austrian naval engineer, Franz Josef Popp. When BMW was incorporated in July 1917, Popp was appointed its first managing director, a post he held until 1942.

BMW's entry into motorcycle manufacturing came as a direct result of the Allied ban on aero-related work in the aftermath of the conflict. Its first efforts began in 1920 with the development of a machine using a proprietary Kurier 148cc two-stroke engine. Named the Flink, it was not a commercial success. Next, in 1921, came the introduction of an engine that would map out BMW's two-wheel future. Designed by Martin Stolle, it was a side-valve, four-stroke horizontal twin. In addition to being employed by BMW to power its own Helios machine, the engine was also supplied to rival firms such as Victoria.

The first true BMW motorcycle was the R32, launched at the 1923 Paris show. This was powered by a direct descendant of the 1922 M2 B15 engine from the Helios. A major difference was that it was mounted transversely, in unit with a three-speed gearbox and shaft final drive – the Helios featured fore-and-aft mounting and chain drive.

The R32 was the beginning of a virtually unbroken line that continues to this day, albeit in updated form. BMW has also produced various singles (today continued with the F650 series) and the K-series of three- and four-cylinder models, which began with the noted K100 in 1983.

From 1928 to 1950, BMW constructed supercharged racing twins for a number of riders, including Georg Meier and Walter Zeller. When Germany became a member of the FIM in 1951 and was unable to employ superchargers, BMW built a special version of the horizontal twin, using overhead camshafts. Called the Rennsport, it found its niche in sidecar racing and went on to win no less than 19 world titles. Drivers included Fritz Hillebrand, Max Duebel, Florian Camathias, Fritz Scheidegger and Klaus Enders.

◀ **1951 BMW R67,** 594cc, overhead-valve, horizontally-opposed twin, 72 x 73mm bore and stroke, original specification, mechanics sound, in need of cosmetic restoration. **£2,300–2,550 BKS**

Introduced in 1951 alongside the R51/3, the 600cc R67 offered a similar level of performance to that of the smaller machine, but produced in a more relaxed manner. The extra capacity resulted in a power output of 26bhp at 5,500rpm, adding only 3mph to the top speed, but the greater torque produced by the bigger engine was noticeable, endearing the model to sidecar users. The R67 was produced from 1951 until 1956.

▶ **1958 BMW R50,** 494cc, overhead-valve twin, period Hoske-type larger-capacity fuel tank and factory optional Denfeld dualseat, otherwise standard specification. **£2,500–2,800 BKS**

The R50/R60 series was launched during 1955 and featured Earles front forks with swinging-arm rear suspension.

1967 BMW R60/2, 594cc, 72 x 73mm bore and stroke, Earles forks, swinging-arm rear suspension, Denfeld dualseat, carrier and crashbars.
£4,000–4,500 BMWC

In all, 3,530 R60 models were built, compared to 17,306 examples of the R60/2.

A known continuous history can add value to and enhance the enjoyment of a motorcycle.

1974 BMW R90S, 898cc, 90 x 70.6mm bore and stroke, dual-disc front brake, pannier frame and rear carrier.
£2,400–2,700 BLM

The R90S was the sporting model of the BMW range between 1973 and 1976. It was famous for its 'smoked' paint finish.

1975 BMW R90S, 898cc, 90 x 70.6mm bore and stroke, fitted with American Rajay turbocharger, 2-into-1 exhaust, aftermarket alloy wheels and fork brace, otherwise original specification.
£2,500–3,000 S

1975 BMW R60/6, 599cc, 73.5 x 70.6mm bore and stroke, drum brakes front and rear, panniers, aftermarket touring fairing and crashbars.
£1,000–1,200 BLM

The R60/6 ceased production in 1976 and was the last of BMW's drum-braked models.

1980 BMW R65, 650cc, 82 x 61.5mm bore and stroke, cast alloy 'spider' wheels, dual-disc front brake, original unrestored condition.
£1,200–1,500 BLM

This machine was also offered in smaller R45 form, both versions being built between 1978 and 1982.

Brough-Superior *(British 1902–39)*

c1913 Brough-Superior WE, 820cc, concours condition.
£10,500–11,500 BKS

The history of the Brough-Superior motorcycle is well documented, but it was the foresight and ingenuity of William Brough that led to the formation of the company. He saw a future for the motorcycle within the motor industry that was emerging in Victorian times. The first all-Brough motorcycle appeared in 1902, and subsequently Brough machines were entered in various reliability trials, proving themselves to be winners. William's son, George rode many of these machines to success and was pictured in 1913 astride a V-twin, an engine configuration he favoured, although his father did not share his conviction. Instead, Brough senior preferred the flat-twin arrangement and went on to produce a range of such engines. In Northern Ireland some years ago, a generator was found being driven by a very rare 820cc Brough V-twin engine. Fortunately, it eventually passed into the hands of a talented Brough club member, whose dedication and skill returned the unit to functioning condition. Coincidentally, when the former Brough-Superior works in Nottingham was being demolished, some Brough enthusiasts visited the site and found that, when the yard was being dug up, various bits of metal had emerged and among them was a casting for the steering head used in the frame of the 1913 V-twin machine. Subsequently, this complete motorcycle was constructed, using many original ancillary cycle parts.

1931 Brough-Superior SS100, 990cc, air-cooled, overhead-valve, V-twin JAP engine, Draper sprung frame, correct engine and frame numbers.
£37,000–41,000 BKS

In 1906, at the age of 16, George Brough completed his first John O'Groats-to-Lands End trial on a machine built by his father. He remembered this event as a miserable experience, but nevertheless it produced a desire to see a new age for the motorcycle. Young George constantly differed from his father over developing technical innovation, and by 1919 he had set up business in Nottingham, where his company produced motorcycles until the late 1930s, using the best components and technology available. His creations were fast, powerful and good-looking, the term 'The Rolls Royce of Motorcycles' soon becoming synonymous with the name Brough-Superior. In 1924, he introduced the famous SS100, each example of which was accompanied by a tag that guaranteed it had reached 100mph on the track. To this day, the SS100 remains the most famous Brough of all, some 3,000 machines of all models having been produced by this famous factory.

Auction prices

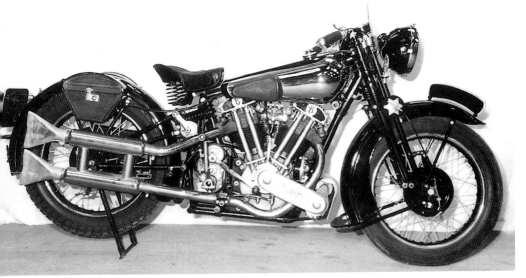

1936 Brough-Superior SS100, 982cc, overhead-valve V-twin, concours condition.
£40,000–44,000 **BKS**

The legendary SS100 was first shown to the public in 1924 and employed an entirely new JAP V-twin engine. The Castle front fork was patented by George Brough and Harold 'Oily' Karslake. From the early 1930s, the SS100 adopted an overhead-valve version of the AMC V-twin and continued to use this engine until production ceased in 1939.

1936 Brough-Superior SS80, 982cc, side-valve V-twin.
£1,200–1,500 **BLM**

The SS80 was the side-valve stalwart of the Brough range. This machine has the Matchless X engine and Norton gearbox.

1937 Brough-Superior SS80, 982cc, side-valve V-twin, complete but in need of restoration.
£9,800–10,000 **VER**

1937 Brough-Superior SS80, 982cc, side-valve V-twin, 85.5 x 85.5mm bore and stroke, matching frame and engine numbers.
£7,200–8,000 YEST

1937 Brough-Superior SS80 Special, 982cc, side-valve V-twin.
£9,000–10,000 TGA

1938 Brough-Superior SS80, 982cc, side-valve V-twin.
£8,500–9,500 TGA

1939 Brough-Superior SS80, 982cc, side-valve V-twin, in need of restoration.
£8,000–9,000 VER

▶ **1939 Brough-Superior 11.50,** 1096cc, side-valve V-twin, 85.7 x 95mm bore and stroke, Norton gearbox.
£10,000–11,000 BLM

The 11.50 was offered from 1933 until Brough ceased production in late 1939. This machine was one of the last motorcycles to be built by the famous Nottingham factory.

BSA (British 1906–71, late 70s–)

At one time, BSA (Birmingham Small Arms) boasted that it was 'the largest motorcycle company in the world'. And there is no dispute that BSA was a major player on the world stage from its earliest days. During the inter-war period, its reputation was built on success in trials, six-day events and early scrambles. In all three disciplines, the Midlands company made a real impact. At the same time, displaying the excellence of its standard product range, it also entered bikes in demonstration tests, including the famous Maudes Trophy.

By the end of the 1920s, the company was able to claim that one in four motorcycles was a BSA, figures helped at the time by such excellent sales performers as the Round Tank and the Sloper.

However, it was not until the end of the 1930s that a motorcycle, or at least a name, arrived that would provide BSA with its enduring image – the Gold Star. Few motorcycles can be everything to everyone, but the 'Goldie' came closer than most – a 100mph lap of the famous Brooklands circuit in Surrey, an Isle of Man Clubman's TT winner, scrambles, trials and, of course, its famous café-racer role – BSA's single could cope with almost anything. Production ceased in 1962, to the regret of its admirers world-wide.

But perhaps BSA's biggest strength was its wide range of models, from such humble machines as the Bantam and C15 to its A-series big-bore twins and finally the Rocket 3 triple.

BSA, together with Triumph, led the export drive. In the immediate post-WWII period, the biggest market for BSA products was the United States, where many thousands of machines were sold until the late 1960s.

But, like the rest of a once great industry, BSA could not cope with the advent of the Japanese steamroller during the 1960s. And as the 1970s dawned, the company floundered, bringing the great marque to its knees. A sad end to Britain's largest motorcycle empire.

1918 BSA K1, 557cc, side-valve single.
£5,000–5,500 **BKS**

A countershaft gearbox enhanced the K1's versatility and allowed the best use to be made of the engine's torque.

1922 BSA V-Twin, 770cc, front-mounted magneto, enclosed chain final drive, caliper brakes, concours condition.
£5,000–5,750 **VER**

1925 BSA Round Tank, 249cc, side-valve, single-cylinder engine, restored, good condition.
£2,000–2,250 **CotC**

1926 BSA B28, 249cc, side-valve single.
£2,000–2,300 **BLM**

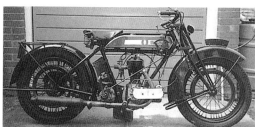

1926 BSA L26, 349cc, side-valve single, 3-speed hand-change gearbox, original rear carrier, tool box and valanced front mudguard.
£1,400–1,600 **BKS**

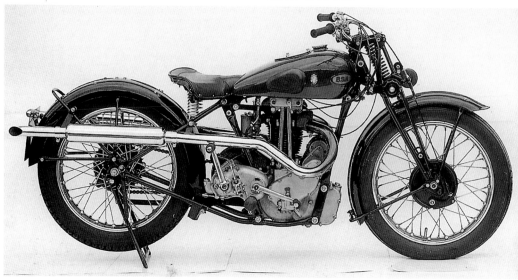

1935 BSA Blue Star, 349cc, twin-port, overhead-valve, single-cylinder engine, high-level exhaust, restored.
£2,100–2,400 **TEN**

◀ **1936 BSA J35-12,** 499cc, overhead-valve V-twin.
£11,000–12,000 **BKS**

Although the majority of 1930s BSAs were singles, the company did market the Model G, a side-valve V-twin, and for the more sporting rider, a smaller overhead-valve V-twin, the 499cc Model J. Debuting in 1934 as the J34-11, the latter became the J35-12 for the following year. Production ceased in 1936, by which time it was being marketed as simply the Model 12.

1947 BSA B33, 499cc, telescopic forks, plunger rear suspension, standard specification.
£2,200–2,500 **PM**

1948 BSA M21, 596cc, side-valve, pre-unit single, 4-speed foot-change gearbox, rigid frame, telescopic forks, restored.
£1,500–1,700 **MAY**

The M21 was manufactured between 1937 and 1963.

Miller's is a price GUIDE not a price LIST

1949 BSA A7, 496cc, overhead-valve, pre-unit twin, 4-speed foot-change gearbox, plunger rear suspension, telescopic forks, chrome tank, pillion pad.
£1,600–1,800 **PM**

1950 BSA A10 Golden Flash, 646cc, overhead-valve, pre-unit twin, 70 x 84mm bore and stroke, telescopic forks, rigid frame.
£2,300–2,600 **TEN**

◀ c1950 BSA ZB32 Gold Star, 348cc, overhead-valve, pre-unit single, 71 x 88mm bore and stroke, alloy head and barrel, 8in front brake, correct specification apart from rigid frame.
£3,000–3,300 **GSO**

In Clubman's or racing guise, ZB-series machines should have a plunger frame. Early Gold Star models are much rarer than the later swinging-arm versions.

1951 BSA B31, 348cc, overhead-valve, pre-unit single, 71 x 88mm bore and stroke, telescopic forks, plunger rear suspension, dualseat.
£1,500–1,800 MAY

1951 BSA M21, 591cc, side-valve single, 82 x 112mm bore and stroke, 4-speed foot-change gearbox, plunger rear suspension, 8in front brake.
£1,000–1,200 MAY

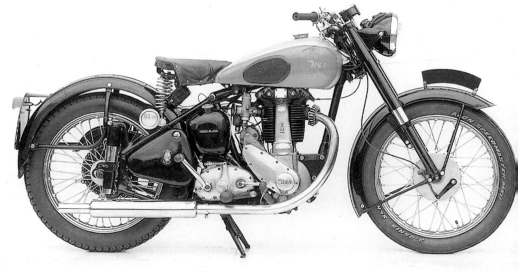

1951 BSA B33, 499cc, overhead-valve, pre-unit single, iron head and barrel, 4-speed foot-change gearbox, telescopic forks, plunger rear suspension, sprung saddle.
£1,300–1,500 TEN

The B33 was highly regarded for its excellent road manners, reliability and the wide range of tasks it could perform.

1951 BSA B34 Gold Star, 499cc, overhead-valve single, alloy head and barrel, telescopic forks, plunger rear suspension.
£3,500–4,000 BLM

1952 BSA B31, 348cc, rigid frame, restored.
£1,600–1,800 H&H

◀ **1951 BSA B31,** 348cc, overhead-valve, single-cylinder engine, iron head and barrel, 71 x 88mm bore and stroke, telescopic front forks, plunger rear suspension, dualseat, restored, good condition.
£1,600–1,900 BLM

1952 BSA C11, 249cc, overhead-valve, pre-unit single, telescopic forks, plunger rear suspension, restored regardless of cost.
£1,000–1,200 BLM

The C11 was developed into the C11G with swinging-arm rear suspension.

1953 BSA B33, 499cc, overhead-valve single, telescopic forks, plunger rear suspension, 8in front brake, headlamp nacelle, sprung saddle, pillion pad, excellent condition.
£1,900–2,300 BLM

1954 BSA D3 Bantam Major, 148cc, 2-stroke single, 57 x 58mm bore and stroke, plunger rear suspension, in need of restoration.
£800–950 H&H

1956 BSA DB32 Gold Star Clubman, 348cc.
£3,500–3,900 BKS

Although the 500cc version of the Gold Star would undergo one more revision prior to production ending in 1962, the DB32 represented the ultimate development of the smaller 350cc variant. As with previous versions, the DB was available with different specifications to cater for the many disciplines of motorcycle sport, as well as for road use. Although a touring variant was listed, the Clubman's specification was arguably the most popular with road riders, offering the ultimate in performance. Equipment included rearset footrests, clip-on handlebars, close-ratio gearbox, straight-through exhaust system and the option of a 190mm front brake, resulting in a machine that had no comparable rivals.

1953 BSA BB34 Gold Star, 499cc, overhead-valve single, swinging-arm rear suspension, touring trim.
£5,400–6,000 BOC

This model was the first of the swinging-arm machines.

1953 BSA A7 Star Twin, 497cc, overhead-valve, pre-unit twin, 66 x 72mm bore and stroke, iron heads and barrels, telescopic forks, plunger rear suspension.
£2,900–3,250 PM

1954 BSA B33, 479cc, overhead-valve single.
£2,000–2,400 BLM

The first year that the swinging-arm frame (from the Gold Star) was made available for the B33 and its smaller brother, the B31, was 1954.

1955 BSA M20, 496cc, side-valve single, 82 x 94mm bore and stroke, telescopic forks, plunger rear suspension.
£1,700–2,000 BLM

1955 BSA M21, 591cc, side-valve single, 82 x 112mm bore and stroke, telescopic forks, plunger rear suspension, 8in front brake, headlamp nacelle, concours condition.
£1,800–2,200 BLM

This 1955 model is the definitive form of the M21. It was popular as a sidecar machine.

1955 BSA B31, 348cc, overhead-valve single.
£1,300–1,500 PS

The B31 was the soft option of BSA's heavyweight 350/500 B-series pre-unit singles. Although lacking power, it was a smooth and comfortable bike.

1956 BSA B31, 348cc, overhead-valve single, fitted with various Gold Star parts including mudguards.
£1,900–2,200 SC

▶ **1956 BSA C11G,** 249cc, overhead-valve, pre-unit single, 4-speed gearbox.
£250–300 PS

The final version of the C11 series, the 'G' benefited from swinging-arm rear suspension.

◄ **1957 BSA B31,** 348cc, overhead-valve, single-cylinder engine, Ariel full-width hubs, swinging-arm rear suspension, headlamp nacelle, standard specification. **£1,500–1,750 PM**

B31 and B33 models first appeared with the swinging-arm frame (originally for export only) in 1954.

1958 BSA Road Rocket, 646cc, overhead-valve twin, 70 x 84mm bore and stroke, completely rebuilt. **£3,600–4,000 CStC**

The Road Rocket was a tuned version of the A10 with a few cosmetic changes thrown in. Today, it is becoming rare.

1959 BSA DB32 Gold Star, 348cc, overhead-valve, pre-unit single, standard B-series gearbox, 8in front brake, alloy rims, touring specification. **£6,000–6,500 GSO**

1959 BSA A7, 497cc, overhead-valve twin, 66 x 72mm bore and stroke, original specification, concours condition. **£3,500–4,000 BLM**

1959 BSA DBD34 Gold Star, 499cc, overhead-valve, pre-unit single, alloy head and barrel, 9:1 compression ratio, Lucas Magdyno, RRT2 close-ratio gearbox, 190mm front brake, original 1½in Amal GP carburettor replaced by easier-to-tune Amal Concentric unit. **£8,500–9,500 BKS**

1959 BSA A10, 646cc, overhead-valve twin, non-standard aluminium wheel rims, 8in single-sided front brake, non-valanced front mudguard, carrier and rear-view mirror.
£1,500–1,750 BKS

1960 BSA C15, 247cc, overhead-valve, unit-construction single-cylinder engine, restored.
£700–900 MAY

c1960 BSA Clubman's DBD34 Gold Star, 499cc, Amal Concentric carburettor, standard gearbox, Commando clutch and rubber belt primary drive, 190mm front brake with Taylor Dow twin-leading-shoe conversion, alloy 'bacon slicer' wheel trims, Super Legerra alloy top yoke.
£6,000–6,600 BLM

1960 BSA A10, 646cc, overhead-valve, pre-unit twin, 4-speed gearbox, full-width hubs, Burgess silencers, standard specification.
£2,350–2,650 CotC

1961 BSA A7 Shooting Star, 497cc, overhead-valve, pre-unit twin, original specification, concours condition.
£3,000–3,500 BLM

The Shooting Star was the sports version of the A7.

1960 BSA A10, 646cc, overhead-valve, pre-unit twin, later BSA/Triumph twin-leading-shoe front brake, alloy rims, otherwise largely original specification.
£3,000–3,400 BLM

1961 BSA B40, 343cc, overhead-valve, unit-construction, single-cylinder engine, 79 x 70mm bore and stroke.
£1,000–1,200 BLM

Based on the 250 C15, the B40 was new for 1961. It differed from the former by having a pushrod tunnel cast into the head and barrel, a valve lifter, 18in wheels and a 7in front brake.

1962 BSA Clubman's DBD34 Gold Star, 499cc, overhead-valve, pre-unit single, 85 x 88mm bore and stroke, RRT2 gearbox, 190mm front brake, concours condition.
£8,000–8,500 **GSO**

1962 BSA Rocket Gold Star, 646cc, overhead-valve, pre-unit twin, touring trim with flat bars, fork gaiters and unit-series headlamp brackets, concours condition.
£6,000–6,500 **GSO**

The Rocket Gold Star is BSA's most sought-after twin-cylinder model.

1965 BSA A65 Star, 654cc, overhead-valve, unit-construction twin, 75 x 74mm bore and stroke, standard specification, good condition.
£1,900–2,300 **BLM**

Introduced in 1962, the A65 and its smaller-capacity brother, the A50, were the first of BSA's unit twins.

1965 BSA D7 Bantam, 172cc, 2-stroke single, 61.5 x 58mm bore and stroke.
£300–350 **H&H**

1966 BSA C15 Star, 247cc, overhead-valve, unit-construction, single.
£900–1,100 **BLM**

The C15 was updated for 1965 with points in the timing cover, an external clutch lever and an improved gearbox. Production ceased at the end of 1967.

◄ **1968 BSA Bantam D14/4,** 172cc, 2-stroke, single-cylinder engine, 4-speed gearbox, completely restored, very good condition.
£600–700 **BKS**

The D14/4 Bantam was a development of the earlier D7 model.

1969 BSA B44 Victor Special, 441cc, overhead-valve, unit-construction single, coil ignition, high-level exhaust, 8in front brake, alloy tank.
£1,300–1,500 CotC

1970 BSA A50 Royal Star, 499cc, overhead-valve, unit-construction twin, 65.5 x 74mm bore and stroke, tri-point screen, mirrors, otherwise standard specification, completely restored, concours condition.
£4,500–5,000 BOC

◄ **1970 BSA B175 Bantam,** 172cc, completely restored 1988/90 at a cost of over £500, little use since.
£400–450 PS

The B175 was the final version of the long-running Bantam family.

1971 BSA A75 Rocket 3 Vetter, 740cc, overhead-valve triple, 67 x 70mm bore and stroke.
£9,000–10,000 BOC

This machine is the original Craig Vetter prototype Rocket 3. It is similar in style to the limited-production Triumph version.

1971 BSA B25 Gold Star, 247cc, overhead-valve, unit-construction single.
£700–800 H&H

The B25 Gold Star was the last of BSA's 250 unit singles.

1971 BSA A50 Royal Star, 500cc unit twin, single carburettor, 4-speed gearbox, twin-leading-shoe front brake, rev-counter, chrome tank, completely restored using mostly original parts.
£4,000–4,400 PC

Some 14,000 A50 Royal Stars were built, and they were the best of the A50 series. This example is one of the last. It was restored from an abandoned machine found under a garden hedge.

Cagiva *(Italian 1978–)*

◄ **1983 Cagiva Aletta Rossa,** 124cc, liquid-cooled, reed-valve, 2-stroke single, 6-speed gearbox, disc front brake, monoshock rear suspension.
£600–700 MAY

Calthorpe *(British 1911–39)*

◄ **1936 Calthorpe Ivory,** 247cc, overhead-valve single. **£2,700–3,000 BKS**

The first Ivory models appeared in 1929, followed in 1930 by the second version, which took the form that characterised the range until the company became linked to Pride & Clarke in 1937. The new model had an ohv, single-cylinder engine laid out in 'sloper' style, with dry-sump lubrication and a three-speed gearbox. Its most notable feature, however, was the ivory livery, which gave potential buyers a radical alternative to the almost universal black and gold schemes worn by rival machines. During 1934, a 247cc model, the Minor, joined the range. Apart from capacity, this was essentially the same as the larger models.

Chater Lea *(British 1900–37)*

Founded during the closing years of the 19th century, Chater Lea turned to the manufacture of lugs and fittings for motorcycle frames around 1900. The firm soon began supplying its high-quality products to the greater part of the emerging British motorcycle industry and eventually began making complete frames. In 1903, it offered its first complete motorcycle. Prior to WWI, Chater Lea motorcycles were fitted with a bewildering range of engines –

more than a dozen different makes, in fact – before the firm began offering its own, alongside those of Blackburne and Villiers, in the 1920s. Motorcycle production was scaled down from 1930 and finally ceased in 1936, after around 5,000 machines had been built.

In its early years, as well as offering completed machines, Chater Lea was happy to provide them in component form for assembly by supplying dealers.

◄ **1910 Chater Lea Model 7,** 738cc, overhead-valve, JAP V-twin engine, complete with all original accessories including Elliott mileometer, Autoclipse and Lucas King of the Road headlamps and Testephone trumpet horn. **£9,000–9,900 BKS**

This machine was assembled by Barnwell's, of Hartley Wintney, Hampshire, for Major Sholto Douglas Wilson. It had a Type 7A frame, Extra No. 2 forks and a 738cc JAP engine. Wilson opted for direct belt drive rather than the standard Model 7's three-speed gearbox and chain, but the machine was updated with those parts in 1912. When Wilson died in 1961, the machine was sold to Harry Mundy, then Technical Editor of *The Autocar*, who gave it to his son Peter. The machine was dismantled and left untouched until 1987, when it was entrusted to restorer Harold Savage for resurrection. The Chater Lea's restoration was completed in 1989.

Clyno *(British 1911–24)*

1912 Clyno Lightweight, 269cc, 2-stroke, unit-construction single, 2-speed hand-change gearbox.
£3,800–4,250 S

Clyno was formed in 1911, in Wolverhampton. Production ceased in 1924, when the company switched to the production of cars. Every Clyno two-stroke was given an engine number that began with the chassis number and type (ie 'L' for Lightweight), ending in two digits indicating the year in which it was built.

Cotton *(British 1919–80)*

◄ **1930 Cotton 350,** 349cc, Blackburne overhead-valve, single-cylinder engine, hand-change gearbox, girder forks, rigid frame.
£4,000–4,500 COEC

The Gloucester based Cotton concern shot to fame with a 1-2-3 in the 1926 Lightweight TT.

Coventry Eagle *(British 1901–40)*

▶ **1931 Coventry-Eagle Tourer,** 196cc, Villiers 2-stroke single, Albion gearbox, chain primary and final drives.
£700–800 BKS

During the early 1930s, the Coventry Eagle range included a quartet of budget-priced, Villiers-powered machines that featured pressed-steel frames and forks.

CZ (Czechoslovakian 1932–)

◀ **1976 CZ Model 632,** 350cc, 2-stroke twin, fully enclosed final drive chain, concours condition.
£750–900 JCZ

CZ (*Ceska Zbroiovka*) was formed in 1918 to manufacture armaments; bikes arrived in 1932. The Model 632 twin had similar cycle parts to the 175cc single-cylinder model of the same era.

DMW (British 1945–71)

1957 DMW Cortina, 225cc, Villiers IH 2-stroke engine, 4-speed gearbox.
£900–1,100 DSCM

DMW (Dawson's Motors, Wolverhampton) began series production in 1950 with a range of small-capacity lightweights using Villiers 10D and 6E engines. The Cortina was produced from 1954 until 1957.

1957 DMW Model 50P, 150cc, Villiers 29C 2-stroke engine.
£900–1,000 DSCM

Douglas (British 1906–57)

1914 Douglas 2¾hp, 348cc, fore-and-aft, flat-twin engine, unrestored.
£5,500–6,000 VER

The original Douglas engine was a fore-and-aft, horizontally-opposed twin, which was mounted in little more than an extended pedal cycle frame.

1914 Douglas 2¾hp, 348cc, restored.
£6,000–6,600 BKS

During the period leading up to WWI, Douglas offered four 348cc models that differed only in detail. The standard model had a single-speed drive. Next in the list came a machine equipped with a two-speed gearbox and clutch, followed by a third that was essentially the same, but had footrests instead of boards. The final 'de luxe' machine was equipped with such refinements as a kickstarter and foot-operated clutch. Interestingly, the beginning of hostilities did not mark the end of civilian motorcycle production, which continued until 1916.

Miller's is a price GUIDE not a price LIST

1915 Douglas Ladies' Model, 348cc, fore-and-aft flat-twin, 3-speed gearbox, clutch.
£5,400–6,000 YEST

1922 Douglas Model HPW22, 348cc, flat-twin engine.
£3,250–3,600 BKS

This machine was displayed in the Rochester Motorcycle Museum, Kent, for a number of years.

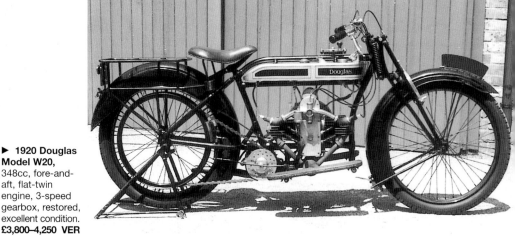

► 1920 Douglas Model W20, 348cc, fore-and-aft, flat-twin engine, 3-speed gearbox, restored, excellent condition.
£3,800–4,250 VER

1923 Douglas Model W, 348cc, fore-and-aft, flat-twin engine, original and unrestored.
£4,000–4,500 VER

1926 Douglas Model EW, 348cc, flat-twin engine.
£5,000–5,500 **BKS**

Designed by Cyril Pullin and launched at the Olympia show of 1925, the EW was intended to benefit from the road tax concessions available to machines of less than 200lb.

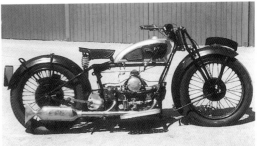

1930 Douglas T6, 596cc, side-valve engine, 68 x 82mm bore and stroke.
£4,000–4,500 **VER**

The final year of production for the Douglas T6 model was 1930.

▶ **1936 Douglas Endeavour,** 500cc, overhead-valve flat-twin, girder forks.
£3,600–4,000 **LDM**

The Endeavour had its cylinders running across the frame, rather than fore-and-aft, as had been the case with Douglas machines up to that time.

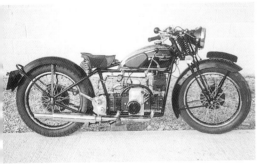

1937 Douglas Aero Twin, 596cc, side-valve, fore-and-aft, flat-twin engine.
£3,300–3,700 **BLM**

The Aero Twin is a post-vintage saddle-tank machine.

1952 Douglas Mark IV, 348cc, overhead-valve, horizontally-opposed twin.
£1,800–2,000 **MAY**

Ducati *(Italian 1946–)*

Ducati's dominant position in WSB (World Super Bike) racing over the last decade is a million miles from its humble beginnings in the 1920s as a radio manufacturer. The great days of this Bologna marque really began in April 1954, when the company head-hunted engineer Fabio Taglioni from its rival FB Mondial, and thus a legend was born. Taglioni, or 'Dr T' as he is affectionately known to his countless admirers around the world, was not only a great designer, but also had a passionate interest in racing.

In the spring of 1955, Taglioni's first new design for Ducati made its debut, and what a debut it was. The 100 Gran Sport (soon nicknamed 'Marianna') simply blitzed the opposition to win its class in that year's Milano-Taranto long-distance road event.

Next came a 125cc single in both valve-spring and desmodromic form. The latter had positive valve operation with two rockers per valve and an extra cam lobe to ensure that the valves were both opened and shut mechanically, rather than being closed by springs. A desmo machine won the first race it contested, the 1956 Swedish Grand Prix.

By 1958, Ducati was well on its way, offering a range of sporting singles (including 175 and 200cc models) and finishing the year as runner-up to MV Agusta in the world championship. In 1959, a youthful Mike Hailwood won his first Grand Prix on a Ducati (the 125cc in Ulster).

The 1960s saw the introduction of the famous Mach 1. However, the company also struck its first serious financial problems, which led to stiffer governmental controls.

The 1970s witnessed the arrival of the famous 90-degree V-twin models, the first being the 750GT of 1971. Victory at Imola, in April 1972, brought considerable prestige, as did Mike Hailwood's victorious return to the Isle of Man TT in 1978. During the 1980s, Englishman Tony Rutter won no fewer than four Formula 2 world titles for Ducati, but once again financial problems almost brought the company to the verge of closure.

The Castiglioni family (owners of the Cagiva brand) gained control of Ducati in 1985. And a decade on, the American group TPG took over.

1957 Ducati 125TV, 124.5cc, 55.2 x 52mm bore and stroke, 4-speed foot-change gearbox, duplex frame, telescopic forks, completely original and unrestored.
£650–750 MAY

This pushrod-engined Ducati was developed from the earlier 98cc model.

1963 Ducati Monza, 248cc, unrestored, non-standard paintwork, converted to Diana (Daytona) specification.
£800–900 IVC

Miller's is a price GUIDE not a price LIST

1965 Ducati Mach 1, 248cc, overhead-camshaft, single-cylinder engine, 74 x 57.8mm bore and stroke, 10.1:1 compression ratio, 29mm Dell'Orto SSID carburettor, alloy rims, white-face Veglia rev-counter, non-standard straight kickstart lever instead of original curved Mach 1 assembly.
£3,000–3,300 PC

1966 Ducati Mk 3, 248cc, overhead-camshaft single, flywheel magneto ignition, US model, 'narrow-case' engine, completely restored, non-standard alloy rims, racing seat, rear shocks, Conti replica silencer and Amal Concentric carburettor.
£2,300–2,800 PC

1970 Ducati 250 Mk 3D, 248cc, unit-construction single, desmodromic valve gear, 74 x 57.8mm bore and stroke, 5-speed gearbox, stainless steel mudguards, standard specification apart from Borrani alloy rims.
£2,650–2,900 PC

1974 Ducati 239 Desmo, 239cc, 72.5 x 57.8mm bore and stroke, desmodromic valve gear, double-sided Grimeca front brake, 35mm Marzocchi forks, non-standard Lucas headlamp, decals for forks, seat and side panels missing.
£2,000–2,300 DOC

The 239cc model was originally built for the French market, where engines under 240cc were subjected to a lower rate of tax.

1975 Ducati 250 Mk 3, 248cc, overhead-camshaft single, conventional handlebars, non-standard fork gaiters and silencer, otherwise standard specification.
£1,300–1,500 IVC

This machine was built in 1974, but not registered until 1975.

1974 Ducati 350 Mk 3, 340cc, bevel-driven, overhead-camshaft single, 76 x 75mm bore and stroke, unrestored, non-standard front mudguard and silencer, seat in need of re-covering.
£1,100–1,300 IVC

1974 Ducati 250 Desmo, 248cc, Brembo front disc brake, rearsets, clip-on handlebars, standard specification, concours condition.
£2,900–3,400 DOC

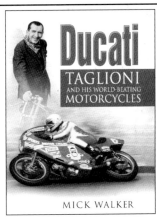

◀ **1975 Ducati Regolarita,** 124cc, piston-port, 2-stroke single, 6-speed gearbox, restored.
£3,200–3,600 BKS

This machine was ridden by Ducati UK's Pat Slinn in the 1975 ISDT in the Isle of Man. It was restored to original specification with parts supplied by Mick Walker.

▶ **1976 Ducati 500 GTL,** 498cc, chain-driven overhead-camshaft, unit-construction engine, electric start, 5-speed gearbox, Brembo dual-disc front brakes, drum rear brake, US export model.
£2,000–2,400 BLM

◀ **1979 Ducati Vento,** 340cc, bevel-driven, overhead-camshaft single, cast alloy wheels, front and rear disc brakes, hydraulic steering damper, completely original.
£2,000–2,500 DOC

Made in the Mototrans factory in Barcelona, the Vento was a Spanish version of the Ducati overhead-camshaft single.

1982 Ducati 500SL Pantah Mk 2, 498cc, desmodromic, unit-construction, 90° V-twin, belt-driven camshafts, 5-speed gearbox, cast alloy wheels, original specification apart from Conti chrome 2-into-1 exhaust system.
£2,250–2,500 PC

1998 Ducati Monster 600, 583cc, desmodromic valve gear, 2 valves per cylinder.
£13,000–14,500 S

This machine was formerly owned by four-times World Superbike Champion Carl Fogarty.

Eclipse *(British 1912–14)*

◄ **1914 Eclipse 4hp Single,** 499cc, single-cylinder engine, 4-speed gearbox, kickstarter, only known surviving example.
£5,000–5,500 TEN

The engineering company Job Day, of Leeds, had a brief affair with motorcycle production during 1912–14, marketing machines under the names Day-Leeds and Eclipse. Single-speed models were offered, or they could be fitted with P&M two-speed gearing or a four-speed gearbox, the gears being driven internally by chains. The engines were of an overhead-inlet/side-exhaust configuration, and production of the machine was on a small scale.

Excelsior *(British 1896–1964)*

1930 Excelsior Model 5, 247cc Villiers 2-stroke engine, 67 x 70mm bore and stroke.
£800–900 VER

Excelsior (UK) as opposed to the American marque of the same name, became involved with motorcycles in 1896. By 1929, when the company gained its first Lightweight (250cc) TT victory, it was well established.

1938 Excelsior Manxman, 348cc, overhead-camshaft single.
£13,500–14,900 BKS

This was the actual works machine submitted for a controlled test by *Motor Cycling* magazine in February 1938. It was ridden by H. G. Tyrell-Smith and Ginger Woods for 16 hours, 31 minutes around the manufacturer's fast track at Donnington Park circuit, completing 520 laps – a distance of 1,000 miles – and averaging 60.65mph. It was also ridden by Tyrell-Smith in the 1938 ISDT, winning a gold medal in the process. The medal still survives in a Spanish private collection.

1954 Excelsior TT2 Talisman, 243cc, 2-stroke twin, concours condition.
£2,000–2,200 ETE

The TT2 was only built in 1954 and 1955. Its engine was of Excelsior's own design.

1955 Excelsior F4 Consort, 99cc, Villiers 4F engine, 2-speed gearbox, girder forks.
£220–250 PS

◄ **1960 Excelsior Super Talisman,** 328cc, 2-stroke twin, twin Amal Monobloc carburettors, completely restored.
£2,000–2,200 ETE

The Super Talisman was very similar to the STT6 Talisman 250 sports model, but it had a larger engine. Both machines had the same cycle parts, including the 6in brakes with full-width hubs.

FN *(Belgian 1901–57)*

◄ **1906 FN Four Cylinder,** 364cc, 4-cylinder inline engine.
£11,300–12,600 TEN

The famous Belgian company, *La Fabrique Nationale d'Armes de Guerre*, was founded in 1889 to produce arms. It began bicycle production in the 1890s, and when motorcycles came along produced its first machine in 1901. FN's chief designer Paul Kelecom laid out his innovative four-cylinder machine during 1904, and it was ridden on a much publicised tour of Europe that year. Production began in 1905. The company was one of the earliest manufacturers to use a four in a series-production motorcycle.

1913 FN Four Cylinder, 364cc, 4-cylinder inline engine, restored, very good condition throughout.
£12,500–13,500 VER

Francis-Barnett *(British 1919–64)*

◄ **1957 Francis-Barnett Falcon 74,** 197cc, Villiers 8E 2-stroke, single-cylinder engine, telescopic front forks, swinging-arm rear suspension, restored, good condition.
£650–800 BLM

Affectionately known as 'Fanny B', the Francis-Barnett marque had a reputation for producing affordable, easily maintained commuter bikes.

Garelli *(Italian 1918–)*

◄ **1977 Garelli KL50,** 49cc, air-cooled, 2-stroke, single-cylinder engine, alloy cylinder and head, Dell'Orto carburettor, full-width hubs, original specification, unrestored.
£350–400 MAY

Gilera *(Italian 1909–)*

◄ **1976 Gilera Arcore 150,** 152cc, overhead-valve, unit single, unrestored, original apart from exhaust and handlebars.
£600–700 MAY

Making its debut in 1972, the Arcore (named after the factory's location) was built in two engine sizes: 125 and 150. Production ended in 1979.

Gitan *(Italian 1950–66)*

1954 Gitan 125 Sport, 123cc, piston-port, 2-stroke single, blade forks, plunger rear suspension, 'factory supplied' trim, excellent condition.
£1,500–1,800 BKS

This model is now very rare.

Dealer prices

Miller's guide prices for dealer motorcycles take into account the value of any guarantees or warranties that may be included in the purchase. Dealers must also observe additional statutory consumer regulations, which do not apply to private sellers. This is factored into our dealer guide prices. To identify dealer motorcycles cross-refer the source code at the end of each caption with the Key to Illustrations on page 167.

Gnome-Rhône *(French 1919–59)*

1934 Gnome-Rhône CV2, 499cc, overhead-valve, horizontally-opposed twin, single carburettor, hand-change gearbox, shaft final drive, pressed-steel frame, tank-mounted instruments.
£4,500–5,500 ATD

Harley-Davidson *(American 1903–)*

1921 Harley-Davidson Model F, 998cc, F-head, V-twin engine, restored.
£6,500–7,500 **BKS**

The first F-head Harleys were introduced in 1909, and in 1912 the company produced a 60.3cu.in (998cc) machine. In 1915, the model was offered with the option of a three-speed gearbox, chain final drive having effectively superseded belt drive during 1913. Nineteen-fifteen had also seen the introduction of electric lighting and improved power output. In this form, the machine was supplied to Allied forces in Europe during WWI, displaying great durability in the harsh conditions of the Western Front. For 1920, the engine was changed significantly, receiving new cylinders, inlet pushrods and flywheels. A side effect of the casting process for the new cylinders was that irregularities occurred, resulting in some machines being shipped with compression plates to equalise the compression of the two cylinders!

1922 Harley-Davidson Model JD,
1200cc, inlet-over-exhaust V-twin.
£14,000–15,500 **S**

Harley-Davidson announced its J-series model in 1917 with a 1000cc (61cu.in) engine; 1922 saw the availability of the larger 1200cc (74cu.in) option.

▶ **1938 Harley-Davidson Knuckle-head,** 1000cc, overhead-valve, V-twin engine, whitewall tyres, studded leather saddlebags, completely restored to concours condition.
£15,500–17,000 **S**

1942 Harley-Davidson WLA45, 750cc, side-valve, V-twin engine, restored, very good condition.
£4,000–4,500 **BKS**

Between 1939 and 1945, Harley-Davidson produced about 88,000 motorcycles for military use. By far the most numerous were the 45cu.in models, which were supplied in large numbers to all of the Allied forces. Two versions were produced, one of them originating in Canada, which was supplied to Commonwealth forces and featured interchangeable front and rear wheels together with provision for a hand-operated clutch, typed the WLC. The other version was the WLA, which was primarily produced for the American forces. With the end of WWII in 1945, a great many Harleys remained in Europe, often being civilianised for sale to a transport-starved public. This machine is just such a conversion.

◄ **1942 Harley-Davidson WLC45,** 750cc, side-valve, V-twin engine.
£3,500–4,000 **BKS**

During WWII, the Harley-Davidson V-twin was used for a wide range of tasks, including patrol and escort work. As with many similar military machines, this WLC45 has been given civilian status, having been fitted with various non-military components, such as the mudguards, and given a new paint job.

► **1948 Harley-Davidson Panhead Springer,** 1000cc, completely restored.
£13,000–14,500 **S**

The last year of the 'springer' front fork was 1948, and this was also the year in which the new 'panhead' style engine appeared. The 1948 model (EL) was the only machine that combined both features.

◄ **c1953 Harley-Davidson WL45,** 750cc, side-valve V-twin.
£4,000–4,600 **BKS**

Production of civilian WL models continued throughout WWII in much reduced numbers, and the model remained available into the 1950s, although by then it was becoming something of an embarrassment to the factory, accounting for about ten per cent of annual production.

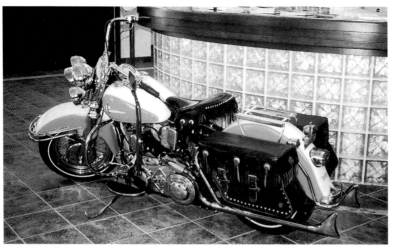

◀ **1958 Harley-Davidson Duo-Glide,** 1200cc, overhead-valve V-twin, 12 volt electrics, swinging-arm rear suspension, dual fish-tail exhausts, completely restored to concours condition.
£6,500–7,300 RM

In 1958, Harley-Davidson replaced the Hydra-Glide with the new Duo-Glide model. Weighing in at 710lb, this new bike was seen as the Cadillac of motorcycles. It featured front and rear crashbars, saddlebags and a single sprung saddle.

1975 Harley-Davidson SX250, 246cc, unused, never registered, only 14 miles recorded.
£2,750–3,300 S

Manufactured in Harley-Davidson's Italian Varese plant (the home of Aermacchi and later Cagiva), the SX250 was one of a series of two-stroke-engined lightweights built with the American market in mind. The machines came in 90, 100, 125, 175, 250 and 350cc engine displacements, but the 250 was the most popular.

1973 Harley-Davidson FXE 1200 Super-Glide, 1200cc, overhead-valve V-twin, electric start.
£5,800–6,500 CotC

Hesketh *(British 1981–)*

1982 Hesketh V1000, 992cc, double-overhead-camshaft V-twin, original factory specification apart from mechanical updates.
£5,600–7,000 BLM

Built in 1982, this machine was not registered until 1985; it was given a factory update by Mick Broom before being put into service.

Honda *(Japanese 1946–)*

oichiro Honda was born in 1906, the eldest on of a village blacksmith in Komyo, ong since swallowed up by the urban sprawl of modern-day Hamamatsu. He left school in 922, taking up an apprenticeship in Tokyo s a car mechanic. Later, he returned to Iamamatsu, opened his own garage business nd, with his new-found source of income, vent motor racing. This came to an abrupt nd after a serious accident at the Tama River ircuit, near Tokyo, in July 1936.

Following this unfortunate incident, Ionda sold his dealership and entered the vorld of manufacturing for the first time with piston-ring company. Then came WWII, vhich saw the Honda organisation making ircraft propellers.

In 1946, Honda returned to the business vorld, setting up the grandly-named Honda 'echnical Research Institute. In reality, this venture was housed in a small wooden hut, n fact little more than a garden shed, on a evelled bomb site on the fringe of Hamamatsu. 'or once, luck was on his side, and after incovering a cache of 500 war-surplus petrol engines, Honda launched himself on the road to motorcycle manufacturing; something he would do with unrivalled success.

The rapid sale of the first Honda bikes encouraged him to move into motorcycle design. Shortly after the incorporation of the Honda Motor Company in 1948, it produced over 3,500 98cc Model D two-strokes, and by 1953 had built 32,000 Model E four-strokes.

Despite increasing production numbers, Honda realised that to survive the company would have to export bikes on a grand scale. To achieve this, his strategy was based on clever advertising, producing world championship winners and building smaller, efficient, but reliable, machines at affordable prices. This recipe for success worked to perfection, and by the mid-1960s Honda's production levels had reached 130,000 bikes per month. That growth has continued to the present time, with not only overseas manufacturing plants being added, but cars, too. And it is the automobile, rather than the motorcycle, that has represented the lion's share of the organisation's annual turn-over since the mid-1980s.

965 Honda CB72, 247cc, overhead-camshaft, twin-cylinder engine, full-width drum brakes, completely restored. **:1,400–1,600 SGR**

The CB72 was the sporting model in the 250cc Honda range during the early 1960s. It was successful in long-distance endurance racing events, such as the Thruxton 500 miles.

◄ **1966 Honda C77,** 305cc, overhead-camshaft, twin-cylinder engine, electric start, direction indicators, 12 volt electrics, pressed-steel chassis, in need of restoration. **£250–300 PS**

The C77 was a larger-engined version of Honda's C-series touring range. These machines, with their squared-off lines, employed pressed-steel chassis, leading-link forks and deeply-valanced mudguards.

◀ **1972 Honda CB750 K2,** 736cc, overhead-camshaft four, 61 x 63mm bore and stroke, electric start, 67bhp at 8,000rpm, 5-speed gearbox, 296mm front disc brake.
£2,300–2,600 PM

▶ **1972 Honda CB450,** 445cc double-overhead-camshaft, twin-cylinder engine, 70 x 57.8mm bore and stroke.
£700–800 BKS

First offered in 1965, the CB450 gained a disc front brake for the 1970 season, having already been given a five-speed gearbox for 1968.

◀ **1973 Honda CL350,** 325cc, overhead-camshaft twin, 64 x 5.6mm bore and stroke, electric start, 5-speed gearbox.
£700–800 PS

The CL350 was built mainly for the American market and featured entwined exhaust pipes for the high-level system but it also had a close-fitting front mudguard.

1973 Honda SS50, 49.5cc, overhead-valve single, 39 x 41.4mm bore and stroke.
£350–400 MAY

The SS50 was first offered in 1967, but with different styling to later models, which featured five speeds and a disc front brake.

1977 Honda CB400F, 408cc, overhead-camshaft four, non-standard fairing and wheels, non-standard paint job, fork gaiters, front mudguard stay missing.
£700–800 MAY

◀ **1951 Ariel KH 500,** 499cc, overhead-valve twin, 63 x 82mm bore and stroke. **£1,800–2,000 H&H**

Designed by Val Page, the Ariel KH twin formed part of a range of singles, twins and fours that was unique among British marques of the 1950s. Like many immediate post-WWII Ariels, the KH not only had telescopic front forks, but also the unusual plunger-type rear suspension that had been devised by Frank Anstey in 1939.

▶ **1955 Ariel VH Red Hunter,** 499cc, overhead-valve, single-cylinder engine, 81.8 x 95mm bore and stroke, telescopic front forks, swinging-arm rear suspension, standard specification. **£2,100–2,400 VER**

The VH Red Hunter was comparable to the Norton ES2 and the BSA B33.

◀ **1957 Ariel LH Colt,** 198cc, overhead-valve single, 60 x 70mm bore and stroke, coil ignition, 4-speed gearbox, plunger rear suspension. **£800–1,000 BLM**

The Colt was offered from 1954 until 1959, being based on the larger-capacity BSA C11G. However, it never achieved comparable sales figures to its BSA Group brother.

▶ **1975 BMW R90/6,** overhead-valve, horizontally-opposed twin, low mileage, 2 owners from new, full history, excellent original condition. **£3,000–3,750 BLM**

The R90/6, like the R90S, was offered between 1973 and 1976. Both were the first BMW production motorcycles to feature five-speed gearboxes.

◀ **1939 BSA M23 Empire Star**, 499cc, overhead-valve single, girder front forks.
£2,000–2,200 BKS

The Empire Star was launched in 1937 and was a good compromise between the rugged reliability of BSA's 'cooking' models and the more highly-tuned Gold Star. It can be seen as the forerunner of the post-war B33 and B31 single-cylinder models.

1960 BSA DBD34 Gold Star, 499cc, overhead-valve, pre-unit single, fitted with correct Clubman's parts, including GP carburettor, swept-back exhaust pipe, Burgess silencer, clip-ons, matching instruments, optional 190mm front brake and alloy rims, concours condition.
£8,000+ GSO

▶ **1961 BSA A10 Super Rocket**, 646cc, overhead-valve, pre-unit twin, completely restored, fitted with later twin-leading-shoe front brake.
£3,000–3,500 BLM

The Super Rocket had the Rocket Gold Star's tuned engine in the standard A-series cycle parts.

◀ **1966 BSA C15**, 247cc, overhead-valve, unit-construction, single-cylinder engine, completely restored to original specification.
£1,000–1,200 MAY

For almost a decade, the C15 was the top-selling British-built 250. Late-model C15s, like this example, had their points on the side of the engine.

◀ **1968 BSA B25 Starfire,** 247cc, overhead-valve single, 67 x 70mm bore and stroke, twin-leading-shoe front brake.
£1,200–1,500 BLM

The B25 entered production for the 1968 model year, replacing the C25 which, in turn, had replaced the long-running C15.

▶ **1969 BSA A75 Rocket 3,** 740cc, overhead-valve triple, 67 x 70mm bore and stroke, 'ray-gun' silencers, US export model with high bars.
£5,200–6,500 BOC

The Rocket 3 differed from its Triumph Trident brother in two main aspects: its styling and the use of inclined, rather than vertical, cylinders.

◀ **1972 BSA A70 Lightning,** 751cc, overhead-valve twin, twin Amal 930 Concentric carburettors, 1 of only 200 made, concours condition.
£8,000–10,000 BOC

The Lightning had a larger version of the 654cc A65 engine, extra capacity being achieved by lengthening the stroke to 85mm. The compression ratio was also increased to 9.5:1, leading to larger jet sizes and a different big-end shell anti-friction coating.

▶ **1921 Douglas Model TS,** 348cc, side-valve engine, outside flywheel, 2-speed gearbox, leather seat and small tool/ oddment holders, restored using original and reproduction parts.
£2,900–3,200 BKS

During the vintage period, Douglas fitted flat-twin engines with fore-and-aft cylinders.

◀ **1961 Ducati Elite,** 204cc, 67 x 57.8mm bore and stroke, twin Silentium silencers, aluminium rear spring covers, chrome tank with 4 parcel hooks, restored to concours condition.
£2,500–2,750 IVC

The Elite was the Bologna based company's first model built mainly for export and was developed from the earlier 175, which made its debut at the end of 1956.

▶ **1964 Ducati 250 Mach 1,** 248cc, overhead-valve, single-cylinder engine, bevel-driven overhead camshaft, 29mm Dell'Orto carburettor, 5-speed gearbox, optional aluminium rims and Veglia racing tachometer, concours condition.
£4,000–4,500 PC

The Mach 1 was the first 100mph production 250 street bike.

◀ **1976 Ducati 900SS,** 864cc, 90° V-twin, bevel-driven camshafts, desmodromic valve gear, 5-speed gearbox, helical-cut primary gears, triple Brembo 280mm disc brakes.
£4,500–5,000 PC

The first of the SS (Super Sport) range, the 750, debuted in 1974; the 900 arrived in the following year. This bike is one of the earliest 'bevel' 900SS models with left-hand gear-change.

▶ **1960 Excelsior S9 Talisman,** 328cc, 2-stroke twin, twin Amal Monobloc carburettors, completely restored.
£2,200–2,500 ETE

The S9 entered production in 1959 and was one of the rarer sights on British roads during the 1950s and early 1960s.

◀ **1952 Harley-Davidson Model FL,** 1200cc, overhead-valve V-twin.
£7,000–7,700 BKS

The overhead-valve 'panhead' engine made its public debut during 1948 and produced 54bhp in 74cu.in form. It replaced the previous 'knuckle-head' engine, offering an increase in performance accompanied by a reduction in engine noise, thanks to the redesigned valve train. In addition, the more extensive use of aluminium in the engine's construction resulted in an 8lb reduction in weight. Initially, the cycle parts were similar to earlier models, but in 1949 hydraulically-controlled telescopic front forks were introduced, providing a substantial improvement in rider comfort.

1970 Honda CB750, 736cc, overhead-camshaft, 4-cylinder engine, 61 x 63mm bore and stroke, 4-pipe exhaust, electric start, 5-speed gearbox, disc front brake, unrestored, concours condition.
£4,000–4,400. BKS

The CB750 was the world's first modern superbike.

◀ **1978 Kawasaki KH250 B3,** 249cc, 2-stroke triple, 45 x 52.3mm bore and stroke, 5-speed gearbox, recent complete restoration.
£1,600–1,900 TGA

Kawasaki built a whole series of three-cylinder models from 250 to 750cc, but the mid-1970s oil crisis led to their demise.

▶ **1956 Matchless G11,** 597cc, overhead-valve, twin-cylinder engine, original specification including megaphone silencers, full-width hubs and dualseat.
£2,500–2,900 BLM

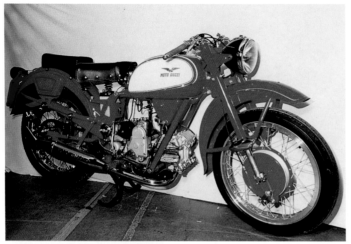

◀ **1955 Moto Guzzi Airone Sport,** 247cc, overhead-valve, horizontal single, 12bhp at 5,200rpm, completely restored.
£3,600–4,000 TDC

Based on the Moto Guzzi 500 Falcone, the Airone was a popular motorcycle in post-war Italy. This particular machine was a concours winner at the 2000 Classic Motorcycle Show at Stafford.

1959 Moto Morini 100 Sbarazzino, 98cc, 4-stroke single, 50 x 50mm bore and stroke, 4-speed unit-construction gearbox, US model imported to UK in 1998, only 1,679 miles from new, original.
£1,000–1,200 MOR

◀ **1972 MV Agusta 350B Sport Elettronica,** 349cc, overhead-valve unit twin, 63 x 56mm bore and stroke, 32bhp at 7,650rpm, 5-speed gearbox, unrestored.
£1,700–1,900 IVC

The 350 was a development of the smaller 250 twin, which had debuted in the mid-1960s.

▶ **1952 Norton Model 7,** 497cc, overhead-valve twin, 66 x 72.6mm bore and stroke, iron cylinders and heads.
£2,800–3,200 BLM

The Model 7 was the first of many Norton twins. It featured a plunger frame, telescopic forks and a new laid-down gearbox.

◀ 1963 Norton 650SS, 646cc, overhead-valve twin, 68 x 89mm bore and stroke, completely restored, original specification apart from alloy rims.
£2,500–2,800 BKS

The 650SS was produced from 1962 until 1968. It won several important endurance races, including the 1962 and 1963 Thruxton 500-mile events.

1926 Royal Enfield 2¾hp Sports, 349cc, side-valve single, recently restored.
£2,500–2,750 BKS

The first 350 Royal Enfield appeared in 1924, using a JAP engine in both overhead- and side-valve form. The JAP engine was replaced for 1925 by Enfield's own motor, while a three-speed Sturmey Archer gearbox was standardised.

◀ 1964 Royal Enfield Interceptor, 736cc, overhead-valve twin.
£3,000–3,300 BKS

Launched in 1948, Royal Enfield's 500cc twin followed orthodox British practice, although its separate barrels and heads, and combined oil tank/crankcase were unusual. A similar 700cc version – the Meteor – arrived in 1952 and for many years was the UK's biggest twin. Both models were revised in 1958, the new 700 adopting the name Constellation. A few years later, the latter was stretched to 736cc, becoming the Interceptor.

► 1966 Royal Enfield Continental GT, 248cc, overhead-valve, unit-construction, single-cylinder engine, 70 x 64.5mm bore and stroke, 5-speed gearbox.
£2,000–2,500 BLM

The Continental GT was a genuine factory café racer. Its gearbox mechanism could be troublesome, but otherwise it was a bike not to be underrated; it was probably Britain's finest road-going 250 of the period. Although not as fast as the Italian Ducati or Japanese Honda, it could still top 80mph.

1924 Rudge Four-Valve,
500cc, 4-valve, twin-port single,
BTH magneto, 4-speed hand
gear-change.
£4,000–4,400 PC

◄ **1912 Scott TT Model,** 496cc,
water-cooled, 2-stroke twin,
open frame, ex-works machine,
restored to concours condition.
£13,500–15,000 WEED

**Scott was an early pioneer in
the field of high-performance
two-stroke engineering.**

► **1929 Sunbeam Model 9,** 493cc,
overhead-valve, single-port single,
80 x 98mm bore and stroke,
hand gear-change, unrestored.
£3,500–4,000 VER

**The Model 9 continued in
production until the 1937
model year.**

1956 Sunbeam S8, 489cc, overhead-valve, inline twin, shaft final drive, original aluminium silencer.
£1,800–2,000 BKS

**Sunbeam introduced the S8 model for the 1948 season, complementing the more formal touring S7.
The machine was of advanced specification, having a rubber-mounted, overhead-valve, inline twin engine.
It also featured modified forks and slimmer tyres, and had a more sporting look.**

1978 Honda CB400F2, 408cc, overhead-camshaft four, 1 x 48.8mm, 5-speed gearbox, completely original apart from aftermarket fairing, concours condition.
1,300–1,500 H&H

1978 Honda CB750F2 Phil Read Replica, 736cc, single-overhead-camshaft four, complete and original.
£1,700–1,900 PC

The special features of this limited-edition model marketed by Honda UK included a racing-style fairing, tank, seat, front mudguard and exhaust system.

980 Honda CBX1000A, 1047cc, double-overhead-camshaft four, 5-speed gearbox, US specification, non-standard exhaust and rear carrier, Comstar wheels.
2,000–3,000 CBX

1985 Honda CD200 Benly, 200cc, twin-cylinder engine.
£210–240 PS

The CD200 was a development of the earlier CD175 model.

Humber *(British 1900–30)*

◄ 1911 Humber, 300cc, side-valve single, belt final drive.
£5,000–5,500 VER

The Humber company had its origins in the cycle industry and built two-, three- and four-wheel powered vehicles from the earliest days. The company also enjoyed considerable racing success, including winning the 1911 Junior TT. After 1930, the firm concentrated on its four-wheel models.

1922 Humber, 50cc, side-valve single, chain final drive, caliper rear brake, drum front.
3,800–4,300 VER

Like Rover, Humber is better known for making cars, but both companies built motorcycles for several years.

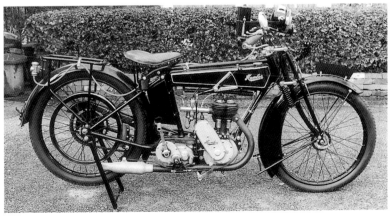

Indian *(American 1901–53)*

The famous Indian marque and its great rival Harley-Davidson were the leading lights of the American motorcycle industry in the first half of the 20th century. Founded in 1901 by two former racing cyclists, George M. Hendee and Carl Oscar Hedstrom, Indian was based in Springfield, Massachusetts.

Indian's first production roadster (it also built a series of very successful racing models in those pioneering days) was a four-stroke single with a vertical cylinder. With this design and the famous V-twin, which debuted in 1907, the marque soon developed a reputation for sophisticated design and excellent quality that would last for many decades.

One of the twins, a 600cc machine, was despatched to Britain in the year of its launch and took part in the 1907 ACU (Auto Cycle Union) Thousand Mile Trial. This event was the forerunner of the world-renowned ISDT (International Six Days' Trial).

With a further eye to its important export market across the Atlantic Ocean, Indian entered no less than four factory-backed riders in the 1911 Isle of Man Senior TT. And what an amazing impression this squad made – Indian machines took the first three places and set the fastest lap in the process. The use of two-speed gearboxes was a major reason for this brilliant success. The result was that Indian became an established name in Europe, resulting in the sale of over 20,000 machines to the Continent in the following year. Then came WWI and the sale of large numbers of motorcycles to the military authorities.

Post-war, the Scout 600cc V-twin arrived in 1919 and proved an instant hit. Designed by Charles B. Franklin, the Scout was renowned for its staying power, witnessed by the factory's advertising slogan: 'You can't wear out an Indian Scout'. This was no idle boast, for a Scout set a new 24-hour road record in 1920, covering 1,114 miles over a closed circuit in Australia.

The scout was followed by the 1000cc Chief in 1922 and the 1200cc Big Chief a year later. The introduction of the mass-produced car in the USA (pioneered by Henry Ford), the application of import tariffs in Britain by the mid-1920s, and the advent of the Depression in 1929 hit Indian hard. However, before this happened, it had acquired the Ace marque.

The financial problems meant that Indian itself was vulnerable, and the company was bought by E. Paul du Pont in 1930. It was not until 1932, however, that the first new model of the revitalised company appeared, and then it was only an economy bike, in the shape of the 31cu.in Scout. Then, in 1933, dry-sump lubrication was adopted for all Indian V-twins. Harley-Davidson did not opt for this feature until 1937, so Indian managed to steal the lead from the main competition. For 1938, high-performance versions of the Scout and Chief were released in recognition of Ed Kretz's much-publicised 1937 Daytona race victory.

With the advent of the 1940s came war rather than peace, and Indian found itself building bikes for the American armed forces once more. After the end of WWII, Indian soldiered on, but profits proved an elusive dream. In 1949, a cash injection was made by British entrepreneur John Brockhouse. Eventually, he assumed outright control, but even this failed to halt the once great company's financial slide, and production was finally terminated in 1953.

1913 Indian V-twin, 1000cc, inlet-over-exhaust V-twin, magneto ignition, pedal starting, footboards.
£15,000–16,500 S

The 1913 Indian models were the first to be offered with both front and rear leaf-spring suspension.

1915 Indian 45cu.in, 700cc, side-valve V-twin.
£8,500–9,500 **BKS**

The 45cu.in model was introduced in 1915 and was well received by the public and military alike.

1918 Indian Powerplus, 997cc, side-valve V-twin engine, completely restored, part of Spanish collection for 19 years, concours condition.
£7,500–8,500 **BKS**

1935 Indian Big Chief, 1200cc, side-valve V-twin, leaf-spring front fork, footboards, later leather-style dualseat and panniers.
£7,000–8,000 **S**

1939 Indian Sport Scout, 600cc V-twin, completely restored to original specification apart from later 1940 engine, 1,200 miles covered since.
£12,000–13,500 **S**

1939 Indian Four, 1270cc, inline four, chain final drive, leaf-spring front fork.
£36,000–40,000 **S**

Auction prices

Miller's only includes motorcycles declared sold. Our guide prices take into account the buyer's premium, VAT on the premium, and the extent of any published catalogue information relating to condition and provenance. To identify motorcycles sold at auction, cross-refer the source code at the end of each caption with the Key to Illustrations on page 167.

◄ **1940 Indian Big Chief,** 1200cc, side-valve V-twin, unrestored.
£10,000–12,000 **PC**

1940 Indian Sport Scout, 600cc, side-valve V-twin, alloy head, iron cylinders, 3-speed hand-change gearbox, Autolite distributor and dynamo, left-hand throttle, right-hand advance and retard.
£10,000–11,000 PC

The Sport Scout was the only Scout model with a sprung rear suspension like the larger Chief.

Cross Reference
See Colour Review

◀ **1946 Indian Big Chief,** 1200cc, side-valve V-twin, non-original headlamp and footboards, completely restored by Indian specialist Bollenbach Engineering.
£17,500–19,500 S

1953 Indian Chief, 1300cc, side-valve V-twin, completely restored by Bollenbach Engineering.
£25,000–30,000 S

The rarest of all Indians, the 1300cc Chief was only built in 1953, the final year of production. Very few were constructed. Unusual features included a telescopic front fork, British Amal carburettor and a shock absorber on the end of the crankshaft to promote smoother running.

James (British 1902–64)

1952 James Comet I, 98cc, Villiers IF engine.
£290–325 PS

1914 James, 225cc, 2-stroke single, magneto ignition, countershaft gearbox, belt final drive with rear brake acting on the belt pulley.
£2,600–2,900 BKS

James was one of the pioneer British motorcycle manufacturers, having begun production in 1902. Early examples of the Birmingham marque were powered by FN engines, but the company quickly added engines of its own manufacture, including 496cc and 596cc V-twins, which became something of a company trademark during the vintage period. James was also an early exponent of the two-stroke engine, making use of both Villiers engines and its own in small-capacity machines.

Miller's is a price GUIDE not a price LIST

Jawa (Czechoslovakian 1929–)

1972 Jawa 90 Roadster, 88.7cc, disc-valve, 2-stroke single, 48 x 49mm bore and stroke, alloy head and barrel, 5-speed gearbox, geared primary drive, fully enclosed final drive chain.
£1,000–1,200 JCZ

1972 Jawa Mustang, 49cc, 2-stroke horizontal single, 3-speed gearbox, concours condition.
£500–600 JCZ

1973 Jawa 90 Roadster, 88.7cc, disc-valve, 2-stroke single, alloy head and barrel, 9.5bhp at 6,500rpm, 5-speed gearbox, geared primary drive, fully enclosed final drive chain.
£1,000–1,200 JCZ

Kawasaki *(Japanese 1962–)*

Unlike its Japanese rivals, Kawasaki can rightly claim that motorcycle manufacturing is only a small part of its global industrial empire. When WWII ended, Kawasaki found its engineering skills in such demand that only one of its many plants was left standing idle. This, too, soon found a niche by producing engine and gearbox assemblies for the emerging motorcycle industry. One of Kawasaki's main customers was Meguro, and it was through this constructor that Kawasaki ultimately became a motorcycle manufacturer in its own right.

Meguro was swallowed up by its larger partner in 1961, and 1962 saw the first model to be adorned with the Kawasaki logo, the 125cc Model B8, a single-cylinder commuter two-stroke. By then, Honda, Suzuki and Yamaha were all well established at home and had already begun their export drives. It is probably true that without its massive financial and industrial might, Kawasaki would have been unable to rise to its current position as an equal member of the Japanese 'Big Four'.

Along the way, it created a series of ground-breaking models: the classic Z1 (1973), the Z1000 (1977), the Z550 (1980), the GPZ1100 (1983), the GPZ900R (1984), the ZXR750 (1989) and the awesome ZZR1100 (1990).

Kawasaki has also designed and built a number of interesting and innovative sporting motorcycles, from the 1969 125cc World Championship-winning disc-valve twin (ridden by the late Dave Simmonds) through to the fearsome 750 H2-R two-stroke triple, campaigned by Yvon Du Hamel at Daytona in the early 1970s. There were also the multi-world-championship-winning inline, two-stroke twins in 250 and 350cc versions. After this came an array of four-stroke fours for endurance and Superbike racing.

1966 Kawasaki W1 650, 624cc, overhead-valve, pre-unit twin, 50bhp at 6,500rpm, full-width alloy hubs. **£3,000–3,500 CKC**

The W1's engine was clearly based on the BSA A10 Golden Flash series.

▶ **1975 Kawasaki 750 H2C,** 748cc, 2-stroke triple, 100bhp at 9,000rpm, 5-speed gearbox, disc front brake, concours condition. **£3,800–4,000 CKC**

1968 Kawasaki 500 H1, 498.8cc, piston-port, 2-stroke triple, 60 x 58.8mm bore and stroke, twin-leading-shoe drum front brake, original specification. **£1,500–1,700 CKC**

1972 Kawasaki Z1, 903cc, double-overhead-camshaft four, 66 x 66mm bore and stroke, 82bhp at 8,500rpm, 5-speed gearbox, disc front brake, concours condition. **£4,000–4,500 CKC**

▶ **1975 Kawasaki H1E,** 498.8cc, 2-stroke triple, disc front brake, completely restored. **£3,000–3,500 VJMC**

1976 Kawasaki Z900, 903cc four, aftermarket 4-into-1 exhaust, dual front disc brakes, stepped dualseat, short front mudguard.
£2,200–2,500 PC

1980 Kawasaki KE125B, 123cc, disc-valve, 2-stroke single, 55 x 51.8mm bore and stroke, 5-speed gearbox, high-level exhaust.
£1,000–1,200 PC

1979 Kawasaki Z1000 Z1–R, 1015cc, double-overhead-camshaft four, 90bhp at 8,000rpm.
£1,500–1,750 PC

The Z1–R was styled very much in the café racer mould popular at the time, with aggressive lines and colour-matched fairing. It also offered a choice of fuel-tank size.

1980 Kawasaki Z400J, 399cc, double-overhead-camshaft four, 6-speed gearbox.
£900–1,000 BKS

1981 Kawasaki Z1000, 1000cc, double-overhead-camshaft four, 4-into-1 exhaust, disc brakes, cast alloy wheels.
£1,100–1,300 MAY

Laverda *(Italian 1949–)*

The very first Laverda motorcycle appeared in 1948, having taken its designer, Francesco Laverda, a year to lay out and construct. Initially, the machine was for his own personal use. It was only when friends in the town of Breganze saw the motorcycle that the idea of a production version was mooted. The originator of the Laverda line had a 75cc, overhead-valve, single-cylinder engine.

Its descendants were to remain in production throughout the 1950s and included a very successful racing variant. The latter machine was a regular class winner in both the Milano-Taranto and Giro d'Italia (Tour of Italy) long-distance road races.

In the 1960s, new designs appeared, including a small-displacement four-stroke scooter (also made under licence by Montesa in Spain) and Laverda's first twin (a 200). But the really big news came at the International Motorcycle Show at London's Earl's Court in the autumn of 1966. That was the venue for the world launch of a brand-new 650cc twin. This, in turn, led to the marque's most revered bike, the production-

racing 750SFC. Although only 549 examples of this specialised machine were built, about 18,500 big twins were made during the 1970s.

A prototype of a new three-cylinder, 1 litre, double-overhead-camshaft model appeared in 1970 and heralded a decade of success, culminating in the 140mph Jota Sportster. Like the twin, the triple was also a winner on the race circuit. A major success was gained in 1976, when Jota-mounted Pete 'PK' Davies won the coveted British National Avon Production series.

Unfortunately, Laverda also made some very costly blunders, notably the V6 superbike and a series of small-capacity two-strokes.

One of the sensations of the 1981 Milan show was the RGS, but even this high-profile model, fitted with the legendary 1000cc triple engine, failed to attract sufficient customers to stave off a financial crisis. This came to a head in the late 1980s, but after a series of failed rescue attempts, Francesco Tognon came to Laverda's aid. The company was relaunched in 1994 with the new 650 Sport, based on the earlier Alpino parallel twin.

1958 Laverda 98 Turismo, 98cc, overhead-valve, unit-construction single, 4-speed gearbox, wet clutch.
£750–850 ILO

1971 Laverda 750 SF, 744cc, double-overhead-camshaft twin, 5-speed gearbox, drum brakes.
£2,200–2,500 IVC

▶ **1973 Laverda 1000 3C,** 981cc, double-overhead-camshaft triple, double-sided drum front brake.
£3,600–4,000 ILO

The 1000 3C was the original version of Laverda's famous triple.

1971 Laverda 750 SF, 744cc, double-overhead-camshaft twin, restored to original specification regardless of cost, 1 owner.
£3,500–4,000 ILO

This 750SF is a first-series model and was imported to the UK from Italy. It features Laverda's own drum brakes.

1983 Laverda RGS Corsa, 981cc, double-overhead-camshaft triple, concours condition.
£3,500–3,750 PC

The RGS Corsa was proposed by British importer Three Cross and was taken up by the factory. It featured big valves, high-compression pistons and fully floating disc brakes. Sixty were imported to the UK, and today the model is much sought-after.

Lea Francis *(British 1911–26)*

Already established as a maker of bicycles of the finest quality, Lea Francis turned to motorcycle manufacture in 1912. Its first model was a refined touring machine notable for its chain drive and two-speed gearbox – at a time when most other machines were belt-driven single-speeders – and featured deeply-valanced mudguards and full enclosure of both drive chains. To save time and reduce development costs, a proprietary engine was used, the chosen power unit being the 3¼hp JAP V-twin of 430cc. Weighing only 220lb and aided by its two-speed transmission, the new machine proved particularly effective at hill climbing, a valuable asset at a time when motorcyclists were

frequently forced to complete ascents by pushing their mounts. The company wasted no time in capitalising on the model's strengths, and in 1913 entered the Scottish Six Days' Trial and the ACU Trial, gaining a gold medal in the former, and gold and silver awards in the latter, in which event one of the 'Leafs' was timed at 53mph. The fully equipped machine was priced at £68.5s, and one of Lea Francis' first customers was the playwright George Bernard Shaw. By 1924, when motorcycle manufacture was stopped in favour of cars, Lea Francis had completed only 1,500 machines. Of these, around 20 are thought to survive, four of which are veterans.

1914 Lea Francis 3¼hp, 430cc, 50° V-twin engine, very rare, restored, excellent condition.
£6,700–7,400 BKS

Levis *(British 1911–40)*

◀ **1921 Levis Popular,** 211cc, 2-stroke single. **£1,200–1,400 H&H**

Levis took its name from the Latin word for 'light', the marque being founded in 1911. The machines were manufactured by Butterfield Ltd of Stechford, Birmingham. The company was a pioneer in the use of the two-stroke engine and also supplied large numbers of engines to the German Zündapp company.

A known continuous history can add value to and enhance the enjoyment of a motorcycle.

▶ **1922 Levis Model S,** 211cc, 2-stroke single, belt final drive. **£2,000–2,200 BKS**

Levis gained an excellent reputation for the good performance and reliability of its two-stroke engines.

◀ **1927 Levis Model M,** 247cc, single-cylinder engine, 67 x 70mm bore and stroke, original. **£2,800–3,200 VMCC**

This full-size 250 made Levis a popular choice with buyers of the period. It cost £29.18s.6d when new.

◄ **1941 Levis A2,**
346cc, overhead-valve,
twin-port single,
70 x 90mm bore and
stroke, high-level exhaust.
£3,600–4,000 PM

Besides its bread-and-butter 2-strokes, Levis
also offered a range of
four-stroke models.

1939 Levis 600, 591cc, overhead-valve, twin-port, single-cylinder engine, 82 x 112mm bore and stroke.
£4,350–4,850 VER

The 600 model was built between 1937 and 1941. It was the largest-capacity machine built by Levis.

Marusho *(Japanese 1966–c70)*

1965 Marusho ST500, 494cc, overhead-valve, unit-construction, flat-twin engine, 4-speed gearbox, shaft final drive,
kickstarter, original specification, chromework in good condition.
£2,000–2,200 S

Matchless *(British 1901–69, 1987–)*

Officially, Matchless could trace its history back to when H. H. Collier built an experimental pedal cycle in 1878, even though his son, Harry, didn't design and build an actual prototype motorcycle until 1899. Brother Charlie scored the marque's first race win in 1901, at Canning Town Track, north London. In 1902, the first production Matchless-powered two-wheeler, fitted with a French 2¾hp de Dion engine, made its debut.

By then, Matchless was well on its way, with Harry Collier winning an award in the ACU 1,000 mile Reliability Trial (the forerunner of the famous International Six Days' Trial). More awards in trials and other branches of motorcycle sport quickly followed. But the really big one came in 1907, when Charlie Collier won the single-cylinder class of the very first Isle of Man TT meeting. In addition to finishing runner-up in the 1908 Single-Cylinder TT, Charlie Collier set a new world record of 69 miles in an hour at the recently-opened Brooklands track in Surrey. He was back on the winner's rostrum at the 1909 TT, having set a new race record of 49mph.

In 1910, a Matchless-built monoplane was flown by Harry Collier, while brother Charlie achieved 84mph at Brooklands. In 1911, Charlie set a new world speed record of 91.31mph, while 1912 saw Matchless build its own engine for the first time.

During WWI, Matchless switched to wartime production, including aircraft parts and bayonets. Some WD motorcycles were also made. When peace returned, only one basic model, a sidecar outfit, was produced.

During the 1920s, both motorcycles and cars were built, while in 1928 the firm became Matchless Motor Cycles. Nineteen-thirty was marked by the beginning of production of the Silver Hawk V-twin, which was the work of Charlie Collier. Not to be outdone, brother Bert created the Silver Hawk V4 in the following year. Also in 1931, Matchless took over the Wolverhampton-based AJS concern.

In 1937, AMC (Associated Motor Cycles) was formed to bring all the Matchless-owned marques under one umbrella organisation. Then, during 1939, production was concentrated on 350cc machines for the British armed services. In 1941, Teledraulic front forks were introduced on WD machines, and in the same year Bert Collier died in a road accident. Worse was to follow when Harry A. Collier died in 1944.

In the immediate post-war period, there were never enough machines to meet demand, while in sport Matchless did well, particularly in trials, winning the prestigious British Experts in 1947 and the Scottish Six Days in 1950.

During the 1950s, AMC acquired several other brands, including James, Francis-Barnett and, most notably, Norton. The Group enjoyed record sales, but 1954 was a sad year, as both Charlie Collier and designer H. J. Hatch died. In 1959, the Matchless G50 racer (based on the AJS 7R) was launched.

If the 1950s were successful, the 1960s were the opposite. Profit soon became loss, and various attempts at jazzing-up the ageing model line-up proved a dismal failure.

By 1966, the financial state of AMC had become extremely serious, leading to the appointment of a receiver. Although the group was taken over by Manganese Bronze and renamed Norton-Villiers, this didn't save the Matchless name. In 1969, the last motorcycle bearing the famous name left the old Plumstead works, much to the despair of enthusiasts the world over.

1924 Matchless L/3, 347cc, side-valve, single-cylinder engine, hand gear-change, completely restored.
£2,400–2,700 **PS**

1928 Matchless Model T3, 497cc, side-valve single.
£2,900–3,250 **VER**

1938 Matchless Model X, 982cc, side-valve V-twin,
85.5 x 85.5mm bore and stroke, foot-change gearbox,
some non-original parts.
£3,500–4,000 **AMOC**

1938 Matchless Model X, 982cc, side-valve V-twin,
original condition.
£6,500–7,200 **BKS**

This machine was formerly owned by sidecar racer
Nigel Rollason and was tested by the late Bob Currie
for *The Classic Motor Cycle* magazine in 1984. During
the test, Currie achieved 85mph.

1954 Matchless G80S, 497cc, overhead-valve single,
iron head and barrel, full-width hubs, 'jampot' rear
suspension units.
£1,800–2,200 **BLM**

**Full-width hubs appeared on Matchless singles for
the first time in 1954.**

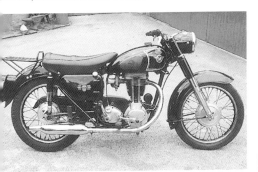

1959 Matchless G3, 348cc, overhead-valve single.
£2,600–2,900 **VER**

The G3 was the economy model of the 350 range.

1958 Matchless G3LS, 348cc, overhead-valve single,
4-speed foot-change gearbox, recently restored,
standard specification apart from rear carrier and mirror.
£2,200–2,450 **PS**

1960 Matchless G9, 498cc, overhead-valve twin, 66 x 72.8mm bore and stroke, incorrect seat, period aftermarket
headlamp peak, unrestored.
£1,900–2,150 **CotC**

MGC *(French 1927–29)*

1931 MGC Sport, 250cc, overhead-valve, twin-port JAP engine, Sturmey Archer hand-change gearbox.
£6,300–7,000 **PC**

The frame, engine cradle, carrier and tank of the MGC Sport are made from a special alloy known as Alpax, a metal that is lighter than aluminium, but enormously strong. There are two main frame members, the top member incorporating the petrol container in one casting (in 1929, *Motor Cycling* referred to this as 'a rather over-sized ostrich egg'). The bottom section of the frame doubles as the oil tank, while the front mudguard is a lockable toolbox. The bike was designed by WWI pilot Giuguet to resemble a swan.

Moto Guzzi *(Italian 1921–)*

1950 Moto Guzzi Falcone, 498.4cc, overhead-valve, horizontal single, 4-speed foot-change gearbox, standard specification apart from speedometer.
£6,000–6,600 **S**

The first year of production for the Falcone was 1950.

1950 Moto Guzzi Airone Turismo, 247cc, overhead-valve, horizontal single, 70 x 64mm bore and stroke.
£1,300–1,500 **PS**

> **Cross Reference**
> See Colour Review

1960 Moto Guzzi Falcone Turismo, 498.4cc, overhead-valve single, 88 x 82mm bore and stroke, 18bhp at 4,300rpm, later model with dualseat.
£3,200–4,000 **IMOC**

A similar Sport version was also built and today is more valuable.

1961 Moto Guzzi Zigolo 110, disc-valve, 2-stroke, horizontal single, 52 x 32mm bore and stroke, original specification.
£1,000–1,200 MAY

The Zigolo 110 was produced from 1960 until 1966; the earlier 98cc version was built between 1953 and 1959.

1974 Moto Guzzi Nuovo Falcone, 498cc, overhead-valve, unit-construction single, 88 x 82mm bore and stroke, electric start, 4-speed gearbox, ex-Public Services machine, some non-original parts.
£2,000–2,200 NLM

1978 Moto Guzzi 254, 231cc four, disc front brake, drum rear, cast alloy wheels, tank-top instruments.
£1,800–2,000 NLM

When Moto Guzzi launched the 254 in 1976, no other company offered anything like it; it was simply revolutionary. It was more often sold with a Benelli badge, but all engines were made in the Guzzi factory.

1980 Moto Guzzi Le Mans Mk II, 844cc, overhead-valve V-twin, 83 x 78mm bore and stroke, 125mph top speed.
£1,600–2,000 BLM

The Le Mans Mk II was more angular than the rounded, racy Mk I, but the SP-type fairing offered more protection for the rider.

1980 Moto Guzzi V35, 346cc, overhead-valve, 90° V-twin, 66 x 50.6mm bore and stroke, shaft final drive, original apart from aftermarket silencers.
£700–800 MAY

1982 Moto Guzzi 1000SP NT, 948cc, 88 x 78mm bore and stroke, 9.2:1 compression ratio, 5-speed gearbox, linked brakes.
£2,000–2,200 NLM

The NT (New Type) SP (Spada in UK) arrived in 1980, and had many improvements compared to the earlier model.

1984 Moto Guzzi California Series II, 844cc, overhead-valve, 90° V-twin engine, excellent condition.
£3,000–3,500 **PBM**

The California Series II made its debut at the Milan show in 1981, going on sale early in the following year.
It featured engine updates from the Le Mans Series III, which was introduced in the same period.

1982 Moto Guzzi V50 Series III, 490cc,
overhead-valve, 90° V-twin engine, 5-speed
gearbox, shaft final drive, SP-type fairing and rear
carrier, unrestored.
£1,000–1,150 **IVC**

1982 Moto Guzzi Le Mans Series III, 844cc, overhead-
valve, 90° V-twin, shaft final drive, unrestored, fitted with
aftermarket fairing, fork brace and rear shocks.
£2,500–2,900 **BLM**

The Series III was the last version of the 850 Le Mans,
before a larger engine was introduced. However,
it was a major redesign, having new bodywork,
exhaust systems and modified engine top end.

1985 Moto Guzzi V35C, 346cc, overhead-valve,
90° V-twin, shaft drive, 18in front and 16in rear wheels,
'western' bars, custom seat.
£1,100–1,300 **NLM**

The last year of production for the V35C was 1985.
The 'C' suffix stood for 'Custom', the machine being
Guzzi's response to the American custom craze that
swept Italy during early 1980.

1990 Moto Guzzi Mille GT, 948.8cc, overhead-valve,
90° V-twin, 88 x 78mm bore and stroke, 18in wire
wheels, unrestored.
£2,400–2,750 **BLM**

The Mille GT was introduced at the 1987 Milan show
and was a return to a more traditional machine after
the poor-selling De Tomaso Studio T5 design of the
mid-1980s.

Moto Morini *(Italian 1937–)*

1956 Moto Morini Briscola, 172.4cc, overhead-valve, unit-construction single, 4-speed gearbox, leading-link front forks, conical front and rear brake hubs, in need of restoration.
£600–700 MAY

The Briscola was one of a trio of 175s launched in 1955, the others being the Tressette and Settebello. Translated, these are 'Trumps', 'Three Sevens' and 'Seven of Diamonds' (all popular card games in Italy).

1960 Moto Morini Corsaro 150, 150cc, overhead-valve, unit-construction single, 4-speed gearbox, original, in need of restoration.
£500–600 MORI

1965 Moto Morini Settebello 175 Turismo, 172cc, overhead-valve, unit-construction single, 4-speed gearbox, touring specification including crashbars, legshields, high handlebars and front mudguard chrome trim, unrestored.
£1,300–1,500 IVC

1969 Moto Morini Corsaro 125, 124cc, overhead-valve, unit-construction single, 4-speed gearbox, wet clutch.
£1,400–1,600 S

'Corsaro' in Italian means pirate. This machine continued in production until 1974 and was also built as a 150.

1968 Moto Morini Corsaro Sport, 123cc, overhead-valve, unit-construction single, matching speedometer and rev-counter.
£800–1,000 NLM

1975 Moto Morini 3½ Sport, 344cc, 11:1 compression ratio, double-sided Grimeca front drum brake, Borrani alloy rims.
£2,700–3,000 NLM

For many Morini enthusiasts, the 3½ Sport is the definitive model, a classic of the mid-1970s.

1974 Moto Morini 3½, 344cc V-twin, Heron combustion-chamber cylinder heads, Grimeca drum brakes front and rear.
£1,400–1,600 BKS

The 3½ was the first Morini V-twin. Although shown at the end of 1971, it did not go on general sale until the beginning of 1973.

1975 Moto Morini 3½ Strada, 344cc, 10:1 compression ratio, touring handlebars.
£2,000–2,200 NLM

Also called the GT and Tour, the original Strada had wire wheels like the Sport, but a single instead of a dual drum front brake. It had a 'softer' camshaft and lower compression ratio, too.

◄ **1976 Moto Morini 3½ Strada,** 344cc, overhead-valve, unit-construction V-twin engine.
£1,800–2,000 NLM

Like the Sport, the Strada was available for a short period with a disc front brake and wire wheels, albeit with chrome instead of aluminium rims, which the Sport offered.

1976 Moto Morini 3½ Strada, 344cc, overhead-valve, unit-construction, V-twin engine, 5-speed gearbox, cast wheels, disc front brake, in need of restoration.
£850–950 IVC

1977 Moto Morini 3½ Sport, 344cc, overhead-valve V-twin, hydraulic steering damper, cast alloy wheels, stainless steel mudguards, concours condition.
£2,000–2,300 NLM

▶ 1978 Moto Morini 250T, 239.29cc, overhead-valve single, 69 x 64mm bore and stroke, rubber-mounted engine, non-standard carrier and top box, excellent condition.
£1,000–1,250 NLM

The 250T was essentially half a 500 V-twin. It was intended primarily for use by municipal and government organisations.

1977 Moto Morini 3½ Strada, 344cc, overhead-valve, unit-construction, V-twin engine.
£1,700–1,900 NLM

For the 1977 model year onward, cast alloy wheels were specified for the 3½ Strada and Sport.

1978 Moto Morini 125, 119.75cc, overhead-valve, unit-construction single, Paiolo front forks, Grimeca front disc brake, 7-spoke cast alloy wheels.
£700–800 MAY

Morini also offered a 250 version of this model.

1979 Moto Morini 500V, 498cc, overhead-valve, 72° V-twin engine, 5-speed gearbox, period rear carrier, fork gaiters and various stainless steel components.
£1,300–1,500 MORI

Later versions of the 500 V-twin came with a six-speed gearbox.

1979 Moto Morini 125H, 119.75cc, overhead-valve single, 59 x 43.8mm bore and stroke, 13.75bhp at 9,000rpm, optional Nisa handlebar fairing.
£1,000–1,100 NLM

The 125H was essentially half a 250 2C V-twin.

1980 Moto Morini 250 2C, 239.5cc V-twin, 26.8bhp at 9,000rpm, 128kg, 87mph top speed.
£1,200–1,400 NLM

The 250 2C was a downsized version of the company's larger V-twin. Little-known and expensive when new, its frame was based on the 125 single with a smaller (13 litre) fuel tank and 31.5mm front forks.

► **1981 Moto Morini 6V,** 498cc, overhead-valve 72° V-twin engine, 6-speed gearbox, triple disc brakes, cast alloy wheels, completely restored to concours condition.
£2,100–2,600 BLM

The '6V' label indicated the use of a six-speed gearbox, which originally had been designed for the Camel enduro model.

1978 MV Agusta Model 216 350 Sport, 349cc, overhead-valve twin, 34bhp at 8,500rpm, 5-speed gearbox, factory optional fairing, concours condition.
£2,500–2,750 **MVA**

1978 MV Agusta America, 790cc, double-overhead-camshaft four, 67 x 56mm bore and stroke, fitted with Magni seat and exhaust, all original parts retained with motorcycle, concours condition.
£18,000–20,000 **MVA**

Neracar *(American/British 1921–26)*

1924 Neracar, 300cc, rare oil-cooled Bradshaw engine, hub-centre steering, in need of restoration.
£4,000–4,500 **VER**

New Hudson *(British 1909–57)*

1915 New Hudson 3½hp, 4-stroke single-cylinder engine, in need of restoration.
£3,000–3,300 **S**

New Hudson built motorcycles for some 30 years from 1903, but during the 1930s turned to the manufacture of Girling brakes. Then, early in 1940, the company returned to the two-wheel scene with an autocycle. Subsequently, this was produced post-war, by which time New Hudson had become part of the massive BSA Group.

1922 New Hudson, 600cc vertical single, chain final drive, drum brakes, flat tanks.
£4,250–4,750 **VER**

> A known continuous history can add value to and enhance the enjoyment of a motorcycle.

New Imperial *(British 1910–39)*

1937 New Imperial 350, 344cc, overhead-valve, unit-construction, inclined single-cylinder engine, girder forks, rigid frame.
£2,800–3,200 MAY

1937 New Imperial Twin Port, 500cc, overhead-valve, unit-construction, inclined single-cylinder engine, foot-operated gear-change.
£3,200–3,600 BLM

1937 New Imperial Model 46, 344cc, overhead-valve, unit-construction, single-cylinder engine, 74 x 80mm bore and stroke, sprung frame, completely restored, excellent condition.
£3,000–3,400 YEST

Nimbus *(Danish 1920–57)*

1936 Nimbus Four, 750cc, inline 4-cylinder engine, shaft final drive, pressed-steel frame, restored.
£3,700–4,100 S

The Nimbus was built in Copenhagen, Denmark.

Norton *(British 1902–)*

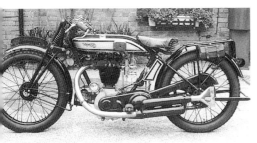

1925 Norton Model 18, 490cc, overhead-valve single, 79 x 100mm bore and stroke.
£7,500–8,500 **VER**

1926 Norton Model 16H, 490cc, side-valve single, 79 x 100mm bore and stroke.
£4,000–4,400 **BKS**

1929 Norton Model 16H, 490cc, side-valve single, 79 x 100mm bore and stroke.
£3,900–4,350 **VER**

One of the many remarkable features that became apparent during the long period of manufacture of Norton motorcycles was the uniformity and longevity of specifications and models. A good example was the Model 16. In 1921, the chain-drive version became the 16H, and this designation continued until 1954. The original machine was fitted with a single-cylinder, 490cc, side-valve engine and a three-speed Sturmey Archer gearbox. A version with high ground clearance was known as the Colonial, while the standard frame, based on the 1920 TT model, was offered for the home market, indicated by the suffix 'H'.

► **c1930 Norton CSI,** 490cc, overhead-camshaft single.
£5,100–5,650 **BKS**

Leading Norton's range as it entered the 1930s was the 490cc, overhead-camshaft CSI. The engine was mounted in a triple-stay frame, providing an easy means of identifying it from the smaller CJ ohc 350.

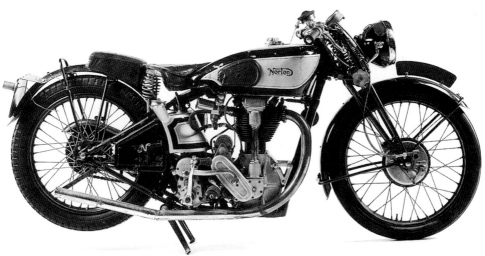

1935 Norton Model 30 International, 490cc, overhead-camshaft, single-cylinder engine, 79 x 100mm bore and stroke, 4-speed foot-change gearbox, completely restored, excellent condition.
£5,200–5,750 **S**

The first overhead-camshaft Norton appeared in the hands of works riders Stanley Woods and Alec Bennett during 1927, marking the beginning of a glorious two decades in Norton's long and illustrious history. During this period, single-cam Nortons gained an astonishing record in competition, at both national and international level. The name International, chosen for the model that replaced the CSI in 1931, demonstrated no immodesty on the part of the company; it simply reflected the outstanding quality of the machines and their success. The new engine was the work of Arthur Carrol, who specified dry-sump lubrication and a magneto positioned at the rear of the cylinder.

1936 Norton Model 18, 490cc, overhead-valve single, high-level exhaust, 4-speed foot-change gearbox.
£3,550–3,950 VER

1935 Norton Model 30 International,
490cc, overhead-camshaft single.
£4,500–5,000 H&H

1937 Norton ES2, 490cc, overhead-valve single,
foot-change gearbox, original, unrestored.
£2,000–2,300 MAY

1946 Norton Model 18, 490cc, overhead-valve single.
£3,100–3,500 PM

1938 Norton ES2, 490cc, overhead-valve single,
girder forks, rigid frame, 'Brooklands can' exhaust.
£3,000–3,500 MAY

▶ **1947 Norton ES2,** 490cc, overhead-valve single,
4-speed foot-change gearbox, telescopic forks,
plunger rear suspension.
£2,000–2,250 PM

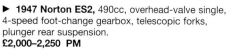

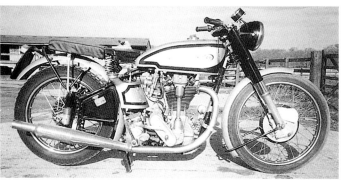

◀ **1949 Norton Model 40
International,** 348cc, overhead-
camshaft, single-cylinder engine,
4-speed gearbox, telescopic forks,
plunger rear suspension, restored,
very good condition.
£4,900–5,400 BKS

**The famous International is one
of the true classic designs of the
British motorcycle industry.**

1949 Norton Big 4, 634cc, side-valve single, 82 x 120mm bore and stroke.
£1,900–2,150 CotC

Mainly sold for use as a sidecar machine, the civilian Big 4 was available between 1947 and 1954.

1953 Norton Model 7, 497cc, overhead-valve twin, dualseat, original, unrestored.
£1,400–1,600 PS

The Model 7 had new pear-shaped silencers for 1953.

 **1957 Norton Dominator 99,** 597cc, 68 x 82mm bore and stroke, original specification, unrestored.
£3,000–3,400 RFC

The 99 was powered by an enlarged version of the overhead-valve 88 engine. Originally purchased new by the famous Scottish racer Jack Gow, this machine has had only one other owner since.

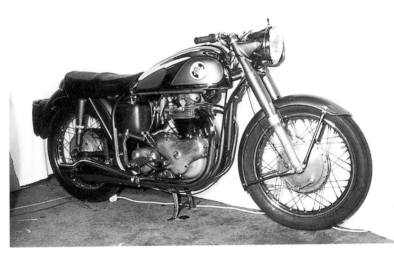

1961 Norton Dominator 88, 497cc, overhead-valve twin.
£3,600–4,000 H&H

1961 Norton Jubilee, 249cc, overhead-valve, unit-construction twin, 60 x 44mm bore and stroke.
£800–900 H&H

Introduced in 1959, the Jubilee was never the big seller that Norton hoped it would be. Later, 350 and 400cc versions were introduced, but they fared no better.

1961 Norton Model 50, 348cc, overhead-valve, single-cylinder engine, slimline Featherbed frame, Roadholder forks, full-width hubs, in need of cosmetic restoration.
£2,000–2,200 PS

The 1961 machine was the final form of the Model 50, which was a smaller-engined version of the ES2.

1963 Norton ES2, 490cc, overhead-valve, single-cylinder engine, 79 x 100mm bore and stroke, Featherbed frame, Roadholder forks.
£2,000–2,500 MAY

This was the final version of the ES2.

1966 Norton 650SS, 646cc, overhead-valve, twin-cylinder engine, non-standard chrome headlamp.
£2,100–2,600 MAY

The 650SS was offered from 1961 until 1968. This model has a single-carburettor head; others had twin carburettors.

1966 Norton N15, 745cc, overhead-valve twin, 73 x 89mm bore and stroke, restored.
£3,200–4,000 BLM

The N15 was essentially a Norton Atlas engine, gearbox, forks and wheels combined with a Matchless frame. It was built primarily for export, notably to the USA. Another version, the P11, had AMC forks and hubs.

▶ **1973 Norton Commando 850,** 850cc, overhead-valve, twin-cylinder engine.
£2,450–2,750 PC

1974 Norton Commando 750 Roadster, 745cc, overhead-valve twin, largely standard apart from modern floating-disc front brake and 4-piston caliper, restored.
£2,650–2,950 CotC

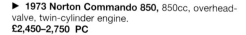

NSU *(German 1901–65)*

Until the company ceased bike manufacture during the early 1960s, NSU was the largest and most powerful motorcycle marque in Germany; bigger than BMW. In the early 1970s, NSU was absorbed into the Volkswagen group, and this meant no more two-wheelers. NSU was also one of the very few manufacturers to have built more than a million of a single model – the Quickly ultra-lightweight.

The NSU story began in 1873, when a pair of engineers, Heinrich Stroll and Christian Schmitt, set up a modest business specialising in the manufacture and repair of knitting machines. Due to its success, the business was relocated to the town of Neckersulm, where the rivers Neckar and Sulm meet; 'NSU' stands for *Neckersulm Strickmachen Union*.

In 1889, the company began to build pedal cycles, and soon this became its main source of income. In 1900, a prototype motorcycle was built, and it went into production in the following year.

Almost from the beginning, NSU's management recognised the importance of motorcycle sport as a proving ground for the company's technology and a marketing tool for its products. As early as 1905, NSU offered a purpose-built competition motorcycle, the 50mph, 402cc *Rennmaschine* (racing machine). In the same year, a sales office was opened in London, British sales exceeding even the most optimistic of forecasts. British riders purchased almost a quarter of Germany's total motorcycle exports in 1906!

There is no doubt that NSU's success in the British market during the early 1900s was a major reason why the company took part in the very first Isle of Man TT races in 1907. Martin Geiger, NSU's British manager, rode one of the German machines to fifth position in the single-cylinder class.

Across the Atlantic, another NSU broke a series of speed records and helped the Germans to establish a foothold in the lucrative US market.

Then came WWI, and for a while sales drives were ditched in favour of armaments. Once the conflict was over, however, NSU started building civilian machines again, with an unfolding line of new models – both for road and track.

During the inter-war years, it was a Briton, in the shape of former Norton man Walter Moore (designer of the famous CSI cammy single), who took on the mantle of chief engineer at NSU. During the 1930s, he developed several new singles, which looked remarkably like his former employer's products, to the extent that it was suggested that NSU actually meant 'Norton Spares Used'.

Moore also did much of the development work on the supercharged parallel twins which, although he left for Britain in 1939, NSU continued to develop until the mid-1950s. In 1956, Wilhelm Hertz set a new world speed record on one of the 500cc twins at Bonneville, Utah, averaging no less than 210.64mph.

During the early 1950s, NSU developed the Rennfox (125cc single) and Rennmax (250cc twin) GP racers, which won several world titles, plus the 250 Sportmax production racer, which also won the world title in 1955. On a visit to Europe in 1954, Soichiro Honda was so impressed with NSU that later he based his own efforts on the German company's products and organisation.

Besides the Quickly series of ultra-lightweights and mopeds, NSU's other top-seller in the 1950s was the Max overhead-camshaft 247cc single.

Another notable NSU project was the series of feet-forward record breakers developed by Gustav Baumm. Although he proved the validity of this highly original approach, he lost his life while testing a racing version at the Nürburgring in May 1955. Prior to the accident, NSU was set to build production versions for street use, but the tragedy caused this scheme to be abandoned.

Although NSU survived the closures that affected many companies within the motorcycle industry during the late 1950s, it never again enjoyed the level of success that it had known in the golden days of the pre-war and immediate post-war periods.

◄ **1949 NSU Fox 4,** 98cc, overhead-valve, unit-construction engine, 50 x 50mm bore and stroke, 5.2bhp at 6,500rpm. **£900–1,100 PC**

The Fox was built in two versions: one fitted with a 98cc overhead-valve, four-stroke engine, the other with a 123cc two-stroke engine.

1953 NSU 98 Italia, 98cc, overhead-valve, unit-construction single, 4-speed gearbox, duplex frame, swinging-arm rear suspension.
£900–1,100 IVC

The Italia was one of many post-war co-operative Italian NSU projects.

1956 NSU Supermax, 247cc, very original.
£3,200–4,000 PC

The Supermax was the final development of the Max theme and was a very refined sports/touring machine

◄ **1958 NSU Quickly-Cavallino,** 49cc, 2-stroke single, 40 x 39mm bore and stroke, 3-speed gearbox, 2.25 x 19 tyres.
£650–800 PC

The Quickly-Cavallino was built between 1957 and 1960; 21,584 examples were produced.

NUT *(British 1912–33)*

◄ **1924 NUT 750SV,** 750cc, side-valve, JAP V-twin engine.
£10,500–11,500 BKS

NUT motorcycles were built in Newcastle Upon Tyne, the city's initials being used to form the marque's name. Winner of the 1913 Junior TT, NUT gained a reputation for producing high-quality V-twin machines, which made use of JAP engines in a variety of capacities.

OK Supreme *(British 1899–1939)*

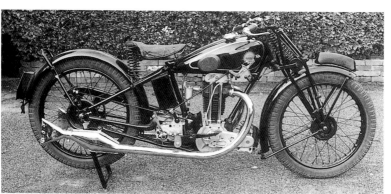

◄ **1930 OK Supreme Twin Port,** 346cc, overhead-valve, JAP single-cylinder engine.
£3,000–3,500 VER

During the 1930s, OK Supreme built a huge range of machines, from a 148cc side-valve single to a 750cc JAP-powered V-twin.

1934 OK Supreme Flying Cloud, 245cc, overhead-valve JAP single, 62.5 x 80mm bore and stroke.
£3,500–3,900 BKS

OK – the 'Supreme' came later – was founded by bicycle maker Humphries & Dawes of Birmingham. The company experimented with powered two-wheelers in the early years of the last century, before exhibiting a Precision-engined range in 1911. When Charles Dawes and Ernie Humphries split, in 1926, the latter continued motorcycle production using the name OK Supreme. The firm entered the Isle of Man TT in 1912, but had to wait for its finest hour until 1928, when OK Supremes filled four of the top six positions in the Lightweight race. The majority of OK's 1930s range was JAP-powered, the exception being the overhead-camshaft models.

Omega *(British 1919–27)*

1920 Omega, 300cc, side-valve, JAP single.
£1,300–1,500 BKS

Initially, Omega employed 269cc Villiers two-stroke engines, but later built its own 170 and 348cc motors. Four-stroke engines were bought in from JAP, Blackburne and Bradshaw.

1919 Omega, 349cc, side-valve, single-cylinder engine, front-mounted magneto.
£1,900–2,100 BKS

Panther *(British 1900–67)*

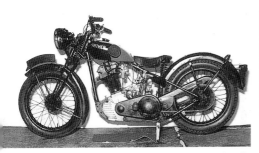

1935 Panther Model 20 Red Panther, 249cc, overhead-valve single, 60 x 88mm bore and stroke.
£600–700 PS

The Red Panther was a cheap and remarkably reliable workhorse, which had a list price of £29.10s.0d when new. It was produced exclusively for Pride & Clarke of south London, who sold large numbers.

1954 Panther Model 65, 249cc, overhead-valve single, 60 x 88mm bore and stroke.
£850–950 H&H

Panther's 250 was considerably updated for 1953, receiving a swinging-arm frame and telescopic forks to provide a much more modern appearance.

Parilla *(Italian (1946–67)*

1960 Parilla Olympia 99, 98cc, overhead-valve, horizontal single, 52 x 46mm bore and stroke, 6.5bhp at 7,200rpm.
£650–750 SGR

The Olympia was produced in both 99 and 125 versions, the larger having a 114cc two-stroke engine.

Premier *(Czechoslovakian 1913–33)*

▶ **1909 Premier V-Twin,** 600cc, side-valve, 90° V-twin, only example known to exist in running order.
£8,500–9,500 BKS

Czechoslovakia (as part of the Austro-Hungarian Empire) was one of the pioneering nations in motorcycle development.

Quadrant *(British 1901–29)*

1924 Quadrant 3½hp, 453cc, inlet-over-exhaust single.
£3,900–4,300 BKS

1903 Quadrant 2hp, inlet-over-exhaust single, inclined cylinder, surface carburettor, completely restored, concours condition.
£6,000–7,000 YEST

Quadrant was at the forefront of motorcycle development during the pioneering days, establishing a new record for the 'End-to-End' run during 1903, a year in which it also introduced its own engines.

Raleigh *(British 1899–1970s)*

1923 Raleigh Model 1, 349cc, 4-stroke single, front-mounted magneto, belt final drive, caliper brakes.
£1,700–1,900 **H&H**

1924 Raleigh Model 12, 800cc, side-valve, 60° V-twin engine, 77 x 88mm bore and stroke.
£8,000–8,800 **BKS**

Raleigh built motorcycles until 1933, when it ceased to concentrate on its pedal cycle business. The Model 12 is now very rare.

◄ **1927 Raleigh Sport,** 495cc, side-valve single, 79 x 101mm bore and stroke.
£2,700–2,800 **TEN**

Rex-Acme *(British 1900–33)*

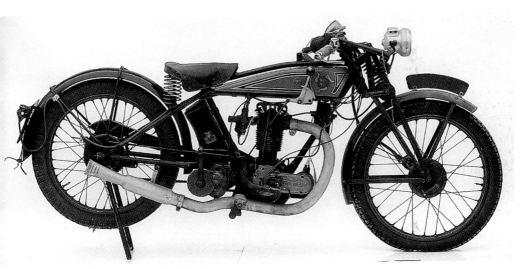

1926 Rex-Acme, 348cc, overhead-valve Blackburne engine.
£3,400–3,800 **TEN**

The Rex Motor Manufacturing Company of Coventry was one of the earliest British motorcycle builders, constructing its first machine in 1900. The name Rex-Acme appeared in 1921.

Rover *(British 1902–25)*

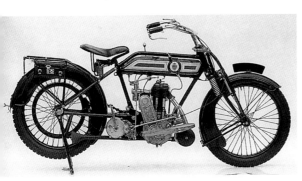

◄ **1919 Rover,** 498cc, side-valve single-cylinder engine, 3-speed gearbox, foot clutch, restored, excellent condition.
£3,600–4,000 **TEN**

Better known for its cars, Rover nonetheless was a leading player in the early days of the motorcycle, producing two-wheelers for almost a quarter of a century, before production ended in 1925.

Royal Enfield *(British 1901–70)*

With its famous slogan, 'Built like a gun', the Redditch-based Royal Enfield concern could trace its history back to the middle of the 19th century. Its first two-wheelers were pedal cycles manufactured during the 1880s. Soon, guns and experimental engines were added. The first complete motorcycle appeared in 1901, with its engine mounted above the front wheel.

From 1912 through to 1920, Royal Enfield produced a variety of machines, but not until 1920 did the company offer a production motorcycle with an engine of its own creation. During the 1920s, a gradual move was made to the exclusive use of Royal Enfield power units, while the machines were designated by type numbers. From 1930, letters were used. Logically, the range for the first year ran from A to K; in time, it would stretch all the way to Z, with a few omissions.

During the 1930s, Enfield built a wide variety of different types, ranging from a 126cc two-stroke to a 1140cc four-stroke V-twin. The company was also something of a pioneer in the traditional British motorcycling establishment, offering engines with four valves per cylinder, unit construction and even all-alloy construction.

During WWII, Royal Enfield's most prolific model was the 125cc Flying Flea, of which some 55,000 were built – several could be packed in a parachute crate for airborne delivery to forces in the field. Not only did the machine prove a big hit with the military, but also when the war ended, Enfield simply changed to black paint and a spot of bright chrome plate and sold them for civilian use!

However, the really big news came in 1949, when Enfield debuted two brand-new models, one an update of a pre-war single design and the other a vertical twin. The 'one-lunger' was the Bullet, a name first used as early as 1933. The prototype had been seen in action in major trials events throughout Great Britain in 1948. The second newcomer was the 500 Twin (later known as the Meteor and, in larger-engined sizes, as the Super Meteor, Constellation and Interceptor).

During the 1950s and 1960s, these two designs formed the cornerstone of Enfield's production, together with a new unit-construction 250 series, which included such models as the Crusader, Super Five and Continental.

In 1963, the company was sold to the E. & H. P. Smith Engineering Group. At the same time, a racing programme got under way, employing riders such as John Hartle, Geoff Duke and Percy Tait, while the designer was Herman Meier. Known as the RE5, the racing machine was fitted with a single-cylinder, two-stroke engine and was a direct competitor to the Greeves Silverstone, Cotton Telstar and DMW Hornet.

By the mid-1960s, however, the entire British motorcycle industry was in rapid decline, from which it was never to recover fully. In Royal Enfield's case, this meant that the company was sold once again, to NVT at Bradford-on-Avon. Production finally halted at the beginning of the 1970s.

Although the Royal Enfield marque had ceased to exist, an overseas factory, Enfield India, continued to build bikes in Madras and does so to this very day. Thus, the Bullet name lives on, machines being exported around the world.

1921 Royal Enfield, 976cc, side-valve V-twin, 2-speed gearbox, all chain drive.
£4,800–5,300 BKS

The powerful Royal Enfield V-twin not only excelled in competition, but also sold well for sidecar use. It was particularly suited to these disciplines because of its two speeds and free engine gearing arrangement, which continued in production from 1912 to the early 1920s. Normally, JAP engines were fitted, but in 1921 these were replaced by a new 976cc, Wolseley side-valve V-twin, built by Vickers to an Enfield design.

1925 Royal Enfield 2¾hp Sport, 349cc, side-valve, single-cylinder engine, restored.
£1,800–2,000 **BLM**

1942 Royal Enfield Model CO, 346cc, overhead-valve, semi-unit, single-cylinder engine, foot-change gearbox, girder forks, rigid frame.
£1,500–1,800 **BLM**

This machine is a former WD model converted for civilian use. There was also a side-valve version, the Model C.

1935 Royal Enfield Model S, 248cc, Miliner compression engine, fully enclosed valve gear, 4-speed hand-change gearbox, blade girder forks, duplex frame, original.
£2,650–2,950 **VMCC**

The Model S cost £35.14s.0d when new.

▶ **1947 Royal Enfield Model G,** 346cc, overhead-valve, single-cylinder engine, 70 x 90mm bore and stroke, telescopic forks, rigid frame.
£1,300–1,500 **PS**

A larger-engined version of this machine, the Model J, utilised the same running gear.

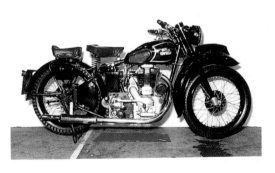

◀ **1956 Royal Enfield Clipper,** 346cc, overhead-valve single, iron head and barrel, telescopic forks, swinging-arm rear suspension, single-sided brakes, original, in need of restoration.
£850–950 **CstC**

The Clipper combined the separate engine and gearbox of the Model G with a swinging-arm frame.

1957 Royal Enfield 500 Bullet, 499cc, overhead-valve, single-cylinder engine, 84 x 90mm bore and stroke, alloy head, full-width hubs, telescopic forks, swinging-arm rear suspension.
£2,000–2,500 BLM

1959 Royal Enfield Big-Head Bullet, 499cc, overhead-valve single, alloy head, chrome tank, updated with twin handlebar-mounted rear-view mirrors and direction indicators.
£3,000–3,500 BLM

◄ **1958 Royal Enfield Crusader Airflow,** 248cc, overhead-valve, unit single-cylinder engine, 70 x 64.5mm bore and stroke.
£1,000–1,250 BLM

The Crusader Airflow was an attempt by Royal Enfield to offer good protection for the rider. In addition to the fairing, the machine was equipped with a front mudguard that fitted around the fork legs for maximum effectiveness.

► **1967 Royal Enfield Continental GT,** 248cc, overhead-valve single.
£2,000–2,400 BLM

The Continental GT was produced from 1964 to 1967. Its café racer style was conceived by the Royal Enfield factory apprentices and proved a great success with buyers. In November 1964, a team of five riders used Continental GTs to travel from John O'Groats to Land's End in under 24 hours.

◄ **1991 Enfield India Bullet,** 499cc, overhead-valve, single-cylinder engine, 12 volt electrics, disc front brake.
£1,000–1,250 BLM

Since the early 1950s, the Bullet has been made in India under licence and has long since outlived its older British brothers. The Madras factory produces both 500 and 350 versions of the machine.

Rudge *(British 1911–40)*

◀ **1919 Rudge Multi TT Roadster,** 499cc, single-cylinder engine, pedal starting, completely restored.
£6,500–7,200 BKS

In 1914, Cyril Pullin won the Senior TT race on his dropped-frame Rudge Multi. Five weeks later, the world was plunged into WWI, which prevented the company from capitalising upon the victory. By 1918, however, the factory was beginning to look toward the production of civilian machines again. Initially, production was confined to models of 499cc capacity, in standard and TT Roadster form. The former retained the pre-war high frame, while the latter had the low frame used by Pullin to win the TT.

1936 Rudge Special, 493cc, overhead-valve, 4-valve, single-cylinder engine, 84.5 x 88mm bore and stroke.
£5,800–6,000 BKS

Nineteen-thirty-six was not a good year for Rudge, fewer than 2,000 machines being sold. Already unstable financially, the firm was placed into liquidation. Fortunately, The Gramophone Company, a subsidiary of EMI, purchased Rudge's assets, and in 1937 production moved from Coventry to Hayes in Middlesex.

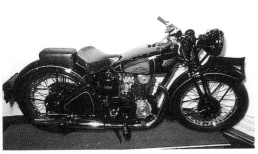

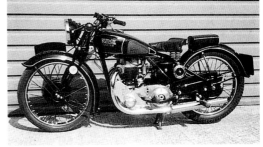

1938 Rudge Rapid, 248cc, overhead-valve single, 62 x 81mm bore and stroke.
£3,500–3,900 REC

1938 Rudge Ulster, 499cc, overhead-valve, 4-valve, single-cylinder engine, 85 x 88mm bore and stroke.
£4,300–4,750 BKS

Introduced in 1928, the Ulster took its name in celebration of the Rudge victory in that year's Ulster Grand Prix. The machine continued in production as the company's flagship model throughout the 1930s, benefiting from ongoing development during that decade. In 1932, it gained a foot-operated gear-change, and in 1933, it received a radial four-valve head, the material changing to aluminium-bronze in 1934. These features would continue into 1937, when the valve gear became enclosed.

◀ **1939 Rudge Special,** 499cc, twin-port, overhead-valve, single-cylinder engine, 4 valves, pent-roof combustion chamber, multi-concours winner.
£10,000–11,000 REC

Scott *(British 1909–late 1960s)*

1913 Scott, 498cc, water-cooled, 2-stroke twin, 2-speed gearbox, telescopic-type front forks.
£17,900–19,700 S

This machine is one of the most famous of all vintage Scotts. It was discovered by the well-known enthusiast Owen Tyler in 1946. On purchasing the machine, Tyler replaced the tyres and spark plugs, and proceeded to ride it for the next 45 years in innumerable Pioneer Runs and similar events. In more recent times, he made the Greatest Combined Age Award his own. Owen Tyler died in 1999 at the age of 99.

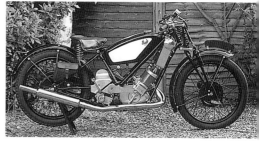

1925 Scott, 498cc, water-cooled, 2-stroke twin, in need of cosmetic restoration.
£3,000–3,500 TEN

Alfred Scott began experimenting with the two-stroke engine during the early part of the 20th century, building his first complete machine in 1908. So advanced was his creation – having a twin-cylinder, two-stroke motor, two speeds and a kickstarter – that for a time it was banned from competition.

Miller's is a price GUIDE not a price LIST

1928 Scott Sports Squirrel, 499cc, water-cooled, 2-stroke twin, 68.25 x 68.25mm bore and stroke, completely restored.
£4,300–4,800 BKS

Although recognisably derived from Alfred Scott's earliest designs, the Scott motorcycle of the 1920s gained steadily in both complexity and weight. A three-speed countershaft gearbox was introduced for 1923, while as a result of the racing programme, there was a new duplex frame and bigger brakes for 1927. For the traditionalists, the old-style two-speed model soldiered on, remaining in production into the 1930s.

▶ **1929 Scott Flying Squirrel Tourer,** 597cc, water-cooled, 2-stroke, twin-cylinder engine, 74.6 x 68.25mm bore and stroke.
£4,000–4,400 BKS

The distinctive 'yowl' of the Scott exhaust note was common to both the 500 and 600cc versions, and in the machine's native Yorkshire Dales was a familiar sound as it roared from valley to valley.

◀ **1929 Scott Squirrel,** 499cc, water-cooled, 2-stroke twin, 3-speed gearbox, rigid frame, girder forks.
£3,000–3,500 PM

Scott owners are among the most enthusiastic in the whole motorcycling clan, even though their favourite marque has been extinct since the late 1960s.

1929 Scott Flying Squirrel Tourer, 499cc, water-cooled, 2-stroke, twin-cylinder engine, 3-speed gearbox.
£5,350–5,950 VER

1930 Scott Sprint Special, 598cc, inclined single-cylinder engine, 73 x 71.4mm bore and stroke.
£10,000–11,000 TEN

Introduced for 1930, the Sprint Special was developed from the Speedway model, having a single seat downtube, while the engine was specially tuned in Scott's competition department. This particular machine was ridden by Miss E. Stuart to win a silver medal in the 1930 Scottish Six Days' Trial.

1938 Scott Flying Squirrel, 499cc, water-cooled, 2-stroke, twin-cylinder engine.
£1,900–2,100 BKS

1947 Scott Flying Squirrel, 596cc, restored, engine rebuilt, 100 miles covered since.
£2,000–2,200 H&H

◀ **1949 Scott Flying Squirrel,** 596cc, full-width brake hubs, telescopic forks, engine rebuilt.
£2,000–2,200 H&H

1959 Scott Flying Squirrel, 596cc, water-cooled, 2-stroke, twin-cylinder engine, Velocette 4-speed gearbox, duplex frame, swinging-arm rear suspension, full-width hubs, dualseat.
£2,700–3,000 BLM

This example of the Flying Squirrel is a late, Matt Holder, Birmingham-built model.

Silk *(British 1974–early 1980s)*

1980 Silk 700S, 660cc, water-cooled, 2-stroke, twin-cylinder engine, 52bhp at 6,000rpm, duplex frame, double-disc front brake.
£2,800–3,100 BKS

Derby based George Silk was responsible for further development of the famous Scott water-cooled twin. The frame components were manufactured by Spondon Engineering. Completed in December 1979, this machine is claimed to be the last 700S built.

> A known continuous history can add value to and enhance the enjoyment of a motorcycle.

Sun *(British 1911–61)*

1914 Sun, 269cc, Villiers 2-stroke, single-cylinder engine, restored, excellent condition.
£3,850–4,250 BKS

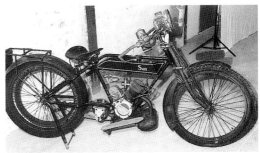

1921 Sun, 269cc, Villiers 2-stroke single, Moss gearbox, unrestored, some parts missing.
£2,100–2,400 BKS

Sun began manufacturing bicycles in 1885 and was based in Aston Brook Street, Birmingham.

Sunbeam *(British 1912–57)*

1923 Sunbeam Model 5, 499cc, side-valve single, 85 x 88mm bore and stroke.
£4,900–5,500 VER

1925 Sunbeam Light Solo, 499cc, side-valve single, 85 x 88mm bore and stroke, fully enclosed rear chain, valanced front mudguard.
£4,900–5,500 VER

1925 Sunbeam 3½hp 499cc, side-valve single, 85 x 88mm bore and stroke.
£5,500–6,100 BKS

Marston Sunbeams were usually built to order. This means that models vary in specification, but frame and engine numbers make it possible to determine the exact model.

1926 Sunbeam Model 2, 346cc, side-valve single, 70 x 90mm bore and stroke, 3-speed gearbox, Lucas mag/dyno ignition/lighting.
£3,000–3,500 SUN

1927 Sunbeam Model 1, 346cc, 70 x 90mm bore and stroke.
£3,600–4,000 VER

1928 Sunbeam Model 5, 492cc, side-valve single, 79 x 105.5mm bore and stroke, Druid forks.
£3,900–4,350 VER

◀ **1928 Sunbeam Model 9 Flat Tank,** 347cc, overhead-valve, single-cylinder engine.
£3,000–3,300 BKS

Bolstered by successes in the ISDT, and in track and long-distance racing events gained by men such as Graham Walker (Murray's father), Charlie Waterhouse and the Italian Achille Varzi, Sunbeam had considerable appeal to enthusiasts who wished to emulate their heroes on the open road.

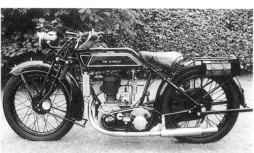

1929 Sunbeam Model 5 Touring, 492cc, side-valve single, fully enclosed front drive chain.
£5,000–5,500 BKS

John Marston was the driving force behind the glory days of the Sunbeam marque. In 1912, then aged 76, he entered the motorcycle arena. His Sunbeam trademark was originally applied to kitchen utensils, and quality paintwork had been a speciality. As a result, the Sunbeam became renowned for its superb finish.

1930 Sunbeam Model 8, 347cc, overhead-valve single, 70 x 90mm bore and stroke.
£4,000–4,400 VER

1930 Sunbeam Model 9 Round Tank, 493cc, twin-port, overhead-valve single, concours condition.
£4,400–4,900 BKS

Sunbeam had begun experimenting with overhead valves on its factory racers in the early 1920s, and these duly appeared on production models in 1924. The new 500 roadster was known as the Model 9, while its race-bike counterpart, which could top 90mph, was designated Model 90. The John Greenwood design was advanced for its day, with a specification that included a crankshaft supported by three ball-bearings, dry-sump lubrication and a primary drive enclosed in a cast alloy chaincase. Power was transmitted by a single-row chain to a three-speed, 'cross-over drive' gearbox with offside power take-off. The Model 9's frame and cycle parts, which had much in common with those of the larger side-valve models, evolved slowly. Sunbeam missed the industry's almost wholesale switch from flat-tank to saddle-tank frames for 1928, and a saddle-tank version of the 9 did not appear until September of that year. Changes to the Model 9's engine were confined mainly to its top end. The early flat-tankers featured a forward-facing exhaust port, a peculiarity that necessitated the adoption of a bifurcated downtube. Later in the 1920s, Sunbeam followed the then-fashionable trend to twin-port heads before reverting to a single-port design in 1934. Pushrod enclosure had arrived by 1930, being followed a couple of years later by partial enclosure of the rocker gear.

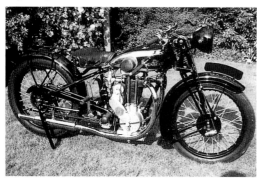

1930 Sunbeam Model 5, 491cc, side-valve single, 77 x 105.5mm bore and stroke.
£2,250–2,750 BLM

1931 Sunbeam Model 10, 344cc, twin-port, overhead-valve single, 74 x 80mm bore and stroke, oil in crankcase, Webb forks, gear lever pivoted on rocker-box cover.
£2,500–2,750 S

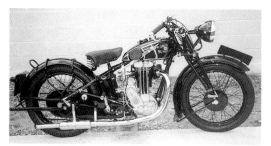

1934 Sunbeam Model 9, 493cc, overhead-valve single, Webb front forks, restored.
£5,400–6,000 BLM

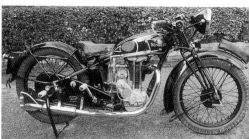

1935 Sunbeam Model 8, 347cc, overhead-valve single, 70 x 90mm bore and stroke, Webb forks.
£3,600–4,000 VER

◀ **1949 Sunbeam S7,** 489cc, overhead-camshaft inline twin, 70 x 63.5mm bore and stroke, 4-speed gearbox, shaft final drive, completely restored, concours condition.
£3,300–3,750 VER

After passing to AMC in 1937, then BSA in 1943, Sunbeam became one of the first British marques to launch a totally new model in the immediate post-WWII period. That machine was the S7.

▶ **1955 Sunbeam S8,** 489cc, overhead-camshaft inline twin, shaft final drive, 19in front and 18in rear wheels.
£1,300–1,500 BKS

First offered in 1949 as an alternative to the Earling Poppe-designed S7, from which it was derived, the S8 was endowed with a more sporting appearance due to the narrower section tyres, slimmer BSA forks and a 7in BSA front brake.

Suzuki *(Japanese 1952–)*

1974 Suzuki GT750K, 739cc, water-cooled, 2-stroke triple, 70 x 64mm bore and stroke.
£1,100–1,300 H&H

Nicknamed the 'Kettle' and 'Water-bottle', the GT750 remained in production from 1972 until 1977. Racing versions were campaigned with considerable success by the likes of Barry Sheene.

1974 Suzuki RE5, 497cc, water-cooled rotary engine, non-standard 'King and Queen' seat.
£3,500–4,000 BKS

The Wankel rotary engine appeared to offer solutions to many of the problems inherent in conventional engine design. However, it proved overweight and over-complex with poor fuel consumption.

976 Suzuki RE5A, 497cc, water-cooled, single-rotor
ɔtary engine, 48bhp at 6,500rpm, 110mph top
ɔeed, non-standard 'King and Queen' seat,
ɔncours condition.
4,500–5,000 **C**

he RE5 was offered between 1974 and 1977,
ut sales never reached expectations. This later
nodel has conventional instrumentation.

1983 Suzuki GSX 1100ES, 1100cc.
£1,000–1,200 IVC

The GSX 1100 and 750 were virtually the same
machines, apart from engine size, and were the last of
the air-cooled, twin-shock sports Suzuki line before the
arrival of the ground-breaking GSX-R series in 1984.

▶ **1984 Suzuki GSX 750 Katana,** 748cc,
ɔouble-overhead-camshaft, air-cooled, 16-valve four,
nti-dive forks, triple discs, twin shocks.
£1,600–2,000 **PC**

ɔroduction of the Katana series began in the early
980s. Its styling, by a European design house,
et it apart from other Japanese superbikes of the era.

Testi *(Italian 1951–83)*

Restored values

The cost of a professional restoration will have an
influence on, but no direct relation to, a motorcycle's
market value. A restored motorcycle can have a
market value lower than the cost of its restoration.

◀ **1980 Testi Champion,** 49cc, Minerelli P4/6, 2-stroke
single, disc front brake, cast alloy wheels, monoshock
rear suspension, matching speedo/tacho, clip-ons,
rearsets, fairing, concours condition.
£1,000–1,200 PC

This machine is one of only 51 examples imported
by Mick Walker Motorcycles of Wisbech in 1980–81.

Train *(French 1913–39)*

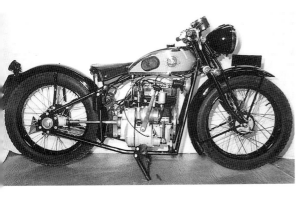

◀ **1930 Train,** 1200cc, overhead-camshaft,
unit-construction, 4-cylinder inline engine,
shaft final drive, restored.
£10,000–11,000 ATD

Train motorcycles were manufactured by
Amicale du Tour du Dauphine, the four-
cylinder model being introduced in 1930.
This machine is the only example known to
have survived, and therefore it will climb in
value in future years.

Triumph *(British 1902–)*

Probably the best-known of all the British marques, the Triumph company was founded by Siegfried Bettmann of Nuremberg, Germany, who moved to Great Britain in November 1883. Bettmann set up the company in Coventry during 1885, originally making pedal cycles, before moving on to motorcycles in 1902.

In 1936, Ariel owner J. Y. 'Jack' Sangster purchased Triumph. This was a major turning point in the company's history, as immediately Sangster employed the talents of the young designer Edward Turner, who earlier had created the Ariel Square Four. Turner not only updated the existing Triumph singles, but also conceived one of the most important motorcycles of all time, the Speed Twin. Although often copied by its rivals over the next quarter of a century, the Speed Twin was never bettered.

In 1951, the company was sold to the BSA Group and a new era began, which saw Triumph become a major dollar earner with not only the latest variant of the Speed Twin, but also such classics as the Tiger 100, Thunderbird and Tiger 110. Finally, at the end of the decade, came the most famous Triumph of all, the twin-carb Bonneville.

But as the 1960s unwound, Triumph, with the rest of the British motorcycle industry, went into terminal decline. Even the introduction of the new 740cc Trident three-cylinder model, in 1968, couldn't prevent Triumph and its parent, BSA, from hitting the financial rocks in the early 1970s.

There followed a workers' co-operative, which failed in the early 1980s, before current owner John Bloor rescued the famous marque in the mid-1980s. Under a veil of secrecy, Bloor set about creating a brand-new model range, with three- and four-cylinder engines. The first of these, built at a new factory on the outskirts of Hinkley, made their debut in the early 1990s. Their success has made Triumph great again.

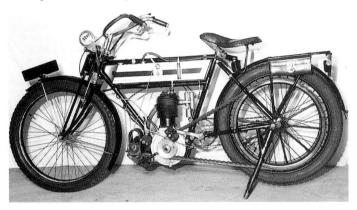

◀ **1910 Triumph Model D,** 499cc, 4-stroke single, belt final drive, pedal starting, front-mounted magneto. **£4,400–4,900 BKS**

The first Triumph motorcycle of 1902 had a Belgian Minerva engine, but within a few years the Coventry marque was building its own powerplants. The company's victory in the 1908 Isle of Man TT single-cylinder race created considerable publicity.

1922 Triumph Ricardo 550, 550cc, overhead-valve, 4-valve, single-cylinder engine. **£5,000–6,000 S**

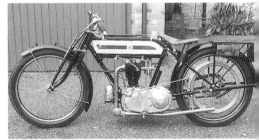

1921 Triumph Model R, 499cc, twin-port, overhead-valve single, 4-valve head. **£7,000–8,000 VER**

▶ **1924 Triumph Model H,** 550cc, single-cylinder engine, 2-barrel carburettor, kickstarter, belt drive, front-wheel speedometer drive, original, unrestored. **£5,000–5,500 VER**

The Model H was very much the economy model in Triumph's 550cc range, offering potential owners the chance to own a Triumph 'on the cheap'.

1924 Triumph 4hp **Model SD,** completely restored.
£3,300–3,700 **BKS**

The 'SD' designation stood for Spring Drive, a name derived from the shock absorber mounted on an extension of the gearbox. The bike was a modernised version of the Model H, featuring a three-speed gearbox of Triumph design as well as a multi-plate clutch, and oil-bath primary chain case and final drive.

1948 Triumph **Speed Twin,** 499cc, overhead-valve, pre-unit twin, 4-speed foot-change gearbox.
£2,400–2,700 **BKS**

Edward Turner's Speed Twin caused a sensation when it was launched toward the end of 1937. Although there had been earlier vertical twins, Turner's creation broke new ground because of its relatively light and compact construction – and its 100mph potential. The 1948 model benefited from a stronger arrangement of eight cylinder-head studs, rather than the six studs found on the original 1937 machine.

A known continuous history can add value to and enhance the enjoyment of a motorcycle.

1949 Triumph **T100,** 499cc, overhead-valve, pre-unit twin.
£5,000–5,500 **VER**

Triumph's first post-WWII twin-cylinder efforts were the Speed Twin and the Tiger 100 (usually shortened to simply T100). These were much as the pre-war bikes with a few changes, notably the adoption of telescopic front forks, which were based on a wartime design and featured hydraulic damping.

1925 Triumph 3½hp **Model R,** 499c, overhead-valve single, 4-valve cylinder head.
£6,500–7,500 **BKS**

Triumph's early output was confined to side-valve machines, but in 1921 the Coventry firm's first overhead-valve model caused a sensation. Based on the existing SD model, whose frame and engine bottom end it inherited, the newcomer sported a four-valve cylinder head designed by Harry Ricardo. Although the 'Riccy' was unsuccessful at the Isle of Man TT races, a works bike ridden by Frank Halford broke the world flying mile record in 1921 with a speed of 83.91mph. The first production models arrived in 1922, equipped with a cast-iron barrel rather than the racer's steel unit, but otherwise were much the same, with paired parallel valves set at 90 degrees in a pent-roof combustion chamber, bifurcated inlet port and separate exhausts. Druid girder forks were fitted until Triumph's own design was ready. Economy rather than outright performance was the road-going Riccy's strongest suit, in excess of 100 miles per gallon being within reach at moderate cruising speeds. Although Rudge went on to make a success of their four-valve designs, Triumph's did not last into the 1930s, being dropped at the end of 1927.

1949 Triumph 6T Thunderbird, 649cc, overhead-valve, pre-unit parallel twin, completely restored.
£4,000–4,500 CotC

The 6T made its debut in September 1949 and featured an enlarged version of the 500 Speed Twin engine. Initially, it was aimed at the American export market.

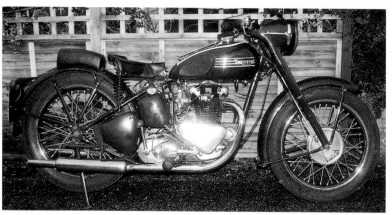

◄ **1950 Triumph 3T,** 349cc, pre-unit, twin-cylinder engine, 55 x 73.4mm bore and stroke, unrestored.
£1,800–2,000 MAY

The 3T was introduced in 1946 and was based on the Speed Twin, although the engine displayed significant differences. It also suffered from a lack of performance because of an inferior power-to-weight ratio.

1950 Triumph 6T Thunderbird, 649cc, overhead-valve, pre-unit twin, restored to original specification.
£4,000–4,400 CotC

1953 Triumph TR5 Trophy, 649cc, overhead-valve, pre-unit parallel twin, 2-into-1 exhaust, telescopic forks, rigid frame, chrome fuel tank.
£3,300–3,700 BKS

Introduced in 1948, the TR5 Trophy was a true all-rounder, a machine that could be ridden to work during the week, but be stripped of extraneous components and used as a weekend competition mount in a variety of motorcycle sports.

◄ **1952 Triumph 5T Speed Twin,** 499cc, overhead-valve, pre-unit parallel twin, 63 x 80mm bore and stroke, sprung hub, period legshields, original specification.
£3,000–3,300 PM

◀ **1953 Triumph T100C,** 499cc, overhead-valve twin, alloy head and barrel, telescopic forks, sprung hub, completely restored, concours condition
£5,800–6,500 PC

A sister machine to this sprung-hub Tiger 100 won the 1952 Senior Clubman's TT, ridden by Bernard Hargreaves. His race average of 82.45mph was the fastest achieved in the race since Geoff Duke's 1949 speed of 82.97mph.

1953 Triumph Speed Twin, overhead-valve, pre-unit twin, iron head and barrel, sprung-hub model, dualseat, concours condition.
£4,000–4,500 MAY

1954 Triumph T110, 649cc, overhead-valve, pre-unit, twin-cylinder engine, iron head and barrel, 8in front brake, swinging-arm frame, restored mid-1990s to standard specification.
£4,000–4,400 CotC

The first year of production for the T110 was 1954.

1956 Triumph TR5, 499cc, overhead-valve, pre-unit parallel twin, close-fin barrel, 2-into-1 exhaust.
£4,300–4,800 VER

For the 1955 season, the TR5's frame was updated with a swinging arm and increased wheelbase as per the T100 model; power rose to 33bhp.

▶ **1956 Triumph T20 Cub,** 199cc, overhead-valve, unit single, 63 x 64mm bore and stroke, 10bhp at 6,000rpm, 4-speed gearbox, plunger rear suspension.
£1,250–1,500 TCTR

The Cub was a development of the 149cc Terrier, which had been launched at the Earl's Court Show in late 1952; the former arrived for the 1954 season. For 1956, the Cub went to a 16in wheel size.

1956 Triumph T100, 499cc, overhead-valve, pre-unit twin, 63 x 80mm bore and stroke, close-fin barrel, single Amal Monobloc carburettor, swinging-arm frame, 8in front brake, headlamp nacelle, original specification.
£4,300–4,800 VER

1958 Triumph 6T Thunderbird, 649cc, non-original siamesed exhaust, all important parts, in need of cosmetic restoration.
£1,800–2,000 MAY

The first year of the 'bathtub' rear enclosure on 650cc models was 1958.

1959 Triumph 5TA Speed Twin, 490cc, overhead-valve, unit-construction, twin-cylinder engine, 69 x 65.5mm bore and stroke, single Amal 375 Monobloc carburettor, original specification.
£1,750–2,000 BLM

The first year of the new Speed Twin with unit engine and 'bathtub' rear enclosure was 1959. It was a development of the smaller 350 3TA Twenty-One.

◄ **1961 Triumph 6T Thunderbird,** 649cc, overhead-valve, pre-unit twin completely restored to original specification, including period aftermarket Craven panniers.
£2,700–3,000 PS

During the late 1950s and early 1960s, the British motorcycle industry had a short love affair with enclosure, which in Triumph's case led to the famous 'bathtub' rear panelwork.

► **1961 Triumph 3TA Twenty-One,** 349cc, overhead-valve, unit twin, 58.25 x 65.5mm bore and stroke, original specification.
£1,800–2,000 CotC

Launched in 1957, the Twenty-One was intended to mark the 21st birthday of the Triumph Engineering Company. Coincidentally, in the USA, a 350cc engine was referred to as having a capacity of 21cu.in. The Twenty-One was the first of Triumph's unit twins.

Velocette *(British 1904–68)*

◀ **1930 Velocette GTP,** twin-port, 2-stroke single, girder forks, rigid frame.
£1,600–2,000 VER

The Velocette marque was established in 1904, but it was not until 1913 that the company (actually called Veloce) established itself with the production of a 206cc two-stroke. The two-stroke series, which eventually included 220 and 250cc models, performed well in most forms of motorcycle sport, as well as proving a hit in the showroom.

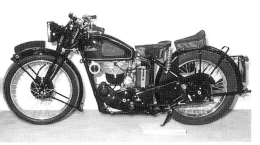

1939 Velocette KSS Mk II, 348cc, overhead-camshaft single, completely restored.
£3,600–4,300 BKS

The first overhead-camshaft Velocette for street use was the Percy Goodman-designed Model K of 1925. The 80mph sports version, the KSS, arrived in 1929, with a revolutionary positive-stop, foot-controlled gear-change, devised by Harold Willis. Introduced for the 1936 season, the KSS Mk II featured many improvements, including a new aluminium cylinder head with enclosed valve gear.

1939 Velocette KSS Mk II 348cc, overhead-camshaft single, 74 x 81mm bore and stroke.
£3,200–3,600 H&H

The KSS was built before and after WWII, the final KSS models being constructed during 1948; its double-overhead-camshaft racing brother, the KTT, survived until 1950. The latter won the first two 350cc World Championships in 1949 and 1950, ridden by Freddie Frith and Bob Foster.

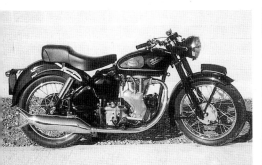

1953 Velocette MAC, 349cc, overhead-valve single, 68 x 96mm bore and stroke, standard specification.
£2,500–3,000 BLM

The MAC and its larger-engined MSS brother were the 'cooking' models of the Velocette overhead-valve range. Nonetheless, they were fine machines, offering a good level of performance compared with competitors from BSA, AJS and Matchless.

▶ **1956 Velocette MAC,** 349cc, overhead-valve, single-cylinder engine, 3 owners, never restored, 3,833 miles covered from new.
£3,500–4,000 BLM

This machine was supplied new with optional chrome tank, pillion footrests and stop lights.

1954 Velocette LE, 192cc, water-cooled, side-valve, 4-stroke flat-twin, 50 x 49mm bore and stroke, hand starting and gear-change, complete but unrestored.
£800–900 MAY

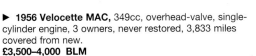

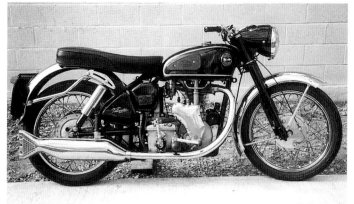

◀ **1956 Velocette Venom,** 499cc, overhead-valve, 4-stroke, single-cylinder engine, 86 x 86mm bore and stroke, restored to original specification.
£3,500–4,000 BLM

The first year of production for this model was 1956. The Venom and the smaller-engined Viper were the high-performance sports models, each having a 7⅛in front brake, full-width hubs and a deep headlamp shell that carried the instruments in its top surface.

1958 Velocette Valiant, 192cc, air-cooled, overhead-valve, 4-stroke flat-twin, 50 x 49mm bore and stroke, 4-speed gearbox, shaft final drive, duplex frame.
£1,200–£1,500 PS

Launched in 1957, the Valiant had an engine based on the LE, but with air cooling, overhead valves and twin carburettors. Unfortunately, it was as expensive as most 250s, but without their extra performance.

1959 Velocette Viper, 349cc, overhead-valve single, 72 x 86mm bore and stroke, 4-speed gearbox, full-width hubs, fishtail exhaust, chrome mudguards, standard specification.
£2,000–2,500 BKS

Unlike the Venom, which had the same bore and stroke measurements of the touring M, the Viper had a shorter stroke than the MAC. With a top speed approaching 90mph, it was as fast as many 500 singles.

1960 Velocette MAC, 349cc, overhead-valve single, unrestored.
£1,500–1,800 BKS

The origins of the 350 MAC can be traced to the pre-war 250 MOV, which introduced the high-cam, overhead-valve design to the Velocette range.

1964 Velocette LE Mark III, 192cc, water-cooled, side-valve flat-twin, 4-speed gearbox, kickstarter, original, good condition.
£600–750 MAY

▶ **1966 Velocette Thruxton,** 499cc, overhead-valve single, twin-leading-shoe front brake, alloy rims, matching speedometer and rev-counter.
£8,700–9,600 BKS

Velocette produced singles that featured strongly in long-distance road races during the 1950s and 1960s, regularly winning their class and running at the front of the pack against machines such as the Triumph Bonneville and Norton Dominator. Toward the end of 1964, Velocette announced a new variant of the Venom, the Thruxton. This featured an Amal GP carburettor, stronger crankcases and a revised lubrication system.

Vincent-HRD *(British 1928–56)*

The original HRD Motors was set up by TT victor Howard Raymond Davies. The company built high-quality, sporting motorcycles, using frames built in-house and JAP engines. The Model 90 featured a single-port, 499cc motor, while the more expensive Super 90 sported a twin-port racing unit and had a top speed approaching 100mph.

HRD could not match profit with the quality of its products and hit the financial rocks during 1927, although bikes continued to be built until early 1928. The name and assets were purchased by Ernie Humphries who, in turn, sold them to a young Cambridge undergraduate, Philip C. Vincent. The latter had long been an enthusiast of the HRD brand and also wanted an established name for the motorcycles he was about to produce. These became Vincent-HRDs. They featured Vincent's own rear suspension and were fitted with Rudge and JAP engines.

Vincent-HRD continued to use proprietary engines until a disastrous showing at the 1934 Isle of Man TT, when its JAP motors proved unreliable. This prompted Vincent to seek the services of the gifted Australian engineer Phil Irving, and together they designed the 499cc engine for the Series A Vincent.

From Vincent's collaboration with Irving came such classic post-war motorcycles as the Comet and Grey Flash singles and, most notably, the legendary Rapide, Black Shadow, Black Lightning and Black Prince 998cc, overhead-valve V-twins.

Both before and after their untimely demise, in 1955, Vincent engines were used to power a number of record-breaking machines. In America, Rollie Free and Marty Dickinson piloted their V-twins to world and AMA (American Motorcycle Association) records on Bonneville Salt Flats. In Britain, George Brown exploited the machines' qualities, creating his renowned Nero and Super Nero sprint bikes to beat the best in the world for over two decades.

◄ **1950 Vincent-HRD Rapide,** 998cc, overhead-valve V-twin engine, 84 x 90mm bore and stroke, 45bhp at 5,300rpm, polished engine casings and main fork arms, non-standard paint finish, 150mph Black Shadow speedometer.
£14,250–15,750 S

The Rapide was the touring model of the V-twin range.

Dealer prices

Miller's guide prices for dealer motorcycles take into account the value of any guarantees or warranties that may be included in the purchase. Dealers must also observe additional statutory consumer regulations, which do not apply to private sellers. This is factored into our dealer guide prices. To identify dealer motorcycles cross-refer the source code at the end of each caption with the Key to Illustrations on page 167.

1951 Vincent-HRD Series C Comet, 499cc, overhead-valve single, sloping cylinder, 84 x 90mm bore and stroke, 28bhp at 5,800rpm, unrestored.
£3,850–4,350 AT

The Comet employed the same bore and stroke measurements as the V-twin models. It was introduced in 1948.

1951 Vincent-HRD Series C Comet, 499cc, overhead-valve single, 6.8:1 compression ratio, Amal 229F/IDV carburettor, Lucas magneto, Miller dynamo, Girdraulic front forks, matching frame and engine numbers, original apart from pattern dualseat and 19in chromed front rim (normally 20in).
£5,400–6,000 VER

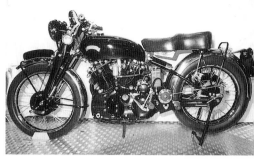

1951 Vincent-HRD Black Shadow, 998 cc, overhead-valve V-twin, 7.3:1 compression ratio, twin Amal 1⅛in carburettors, 55bhp at 5,700rpm, 125mph top speed, original specification including 150mph speedometer, completely restored to concours condition.
£15,800–16,500 CNI

▶ **1952 Vincent-HRD Series C Comet,** 499cc, overhead-valve single, standard specification apart from period tank cover and bar-end mirror.
£5,000–5,500 BKS

The Comet had essentially the same cycle parts as the Rapide, while the engine was effectively half of the V-twin engine. For the 500cc model, the separate gearbox was of Burman manufacture.

1954 Vincent-HRD Black Shadow, 998cc, overhead-valve V-twin, engine rebuilt by Tony Maughan in Australia.
£13,000–14,500 COYS

Official road testers of the day achieved different speeds for the Black Shadow. For example, *Motor Cycling* recorded 122mph, while *American Cycles* managed 128mph. The majority of Vincent experts agree on 125mph as a sensible figure for an example in A1 trim.

1955 Vincent Black Prince, 998cc, overhead-valve V-twin.
£10,000–11,000 BKS

In September 1955, when it was revealed that production of Vincent machines would cease, the news stunned the motorcycling world; it had been decided that the firm's future lay in more profitable lines of manufacture, and just 100 more of the fabulous V-twins would be completed. At the time, Vincent's final twin, the Series D, had been in production for only six months. It had been Philip Vincent's belief that provision of ample weather protection, combined with enclosure of engine and gearbox, would make the Series D the ultimate 'gentleman's motorcycle', although delayed delivery of the fibreglass panels, plus continued demand for traditionally-styled models, resulted in over half the production having no enclosure. The enclosed Rapide and Black Shadow were known as Black Knight and Black Prince respectively. This particular Black Prince was the last of that final batch of 100 machines. It was acquired in 1974, having been dismantled and stored for some time, preserved in buckets of oil. Over the next two years, it was rebuilt using the original parts, and in 1976 entered use again on a daily basis. Then, in the mid-1980s, it was taken off the road and exhibited at the National Motor Museum, Beaulieu, until 1993.

1955 Vincent-HRD Series D Black Shadow. 998cc, overhead-valve V-twin.
£16,000–17,500 BKS

The Series D Black Shadow was the last model to be produced by Vincent. Some 50 of these machines were built, around half of total Series D production; the other models were the fully-enclosed Black Prince and the Black Knight.

Whizzer *(American 1947–54)*

1951 Whizzer Pacemaker, 200cc, pedal starting, belt final drive, concours condition.
£2,500–3,000 S

The Whizzer was exactly what it appeared to be: an American pedal cycle fitted with an engine. In Europe at that time, the equivalent autocycles were usually powered by 50cc motors.

1952 Whizzer, 200cc, completely restored, standard specification apart from Mikuni carburettor to ease starting.
£1,100–1,300 S

This model was built on a Flyer bicycle frame, using the Schwinn spring-fork design.

Yamaha *(Japanese 1954–)*

Formed in 1954, the Yamaha motorcycle marque has pursued an unwavering commitment to racing, which has included both official works entries and customer 'over-the-counter' machines.

Although Yamaha only began building motorcycles in the early 1950s, its origins actually go back to the 19th century, when Torakusa Yamaha began repairing organs in 1887. This set him on a course that eventually saw his company, Nippon Gakki, become one of the world's leading manufacturers of musical instruments. Before the turn of the century, Nippon Gakki had become not only a major supplier on the home market, but also had begun an export drive, which included shipping some 80 organs to Britain in 1892.

Although Torakusa Yamaha died in 1916, Nippon Gakki continued to expand, even when its production facilities were badly damaged by Allied bombing in 1945. The management and work-force managed to struggle back into

making musical instruments once more in 1948.

During 1950, control of the company passed to Genichi Kawakami, then 38 years old. One of his first moves was to take the decision to begin motorcycle manufacture, even though the company had no previous experience in this field. Its first model closely followed the German DKW RT125, as did machines built by many other companies, including BSA and Harley-Davidson.

From this initial effort came a long line of ever-improving two-stroke models, culminating in the RD-series during the 1970s and later the LC (Liquid Cooled) range. Running parallel to these developments was a competition programme based on similar models – the TD and TZ.

Like Suzuki, in more recent times Yamaha has switched to predominantly four-stroke-engined bikes, but still builds a number of two-stroke lightweights. Moreover, at the beginning of the 21st century, the company has won great acclaim by producing trend-setting sportsters, such as the R1 and R6.

◀ **1968 Yamaha YA6,** 124cc, disc-valve, 2-stroke single, pumped lubrication, full-width alloy hubs, pressed-steel swinging-arm frame, telescopic forks.
£600–700 PC

The YA6 was one of Yamaha's early models, and it was exported to Europe and North America in small numbers. It was a very modern design – probably the best of the Japanese two-strokes.

◄ **1978 Yamaha RD 250E,** 247cc, 2-stroke twin, 54 x 54mm bore and stroke, 30bhp at 7,500rpm, CDI magneto ignition, 6-speed gearbox. **£450–600 PS**

First offered in 1973, the RD250 was produced until 1979. The Series E was the final type, being offered in 1978/79 with front and rear disc brakes and cast alloy wheels.

► **1979 Yamaha FS1E,** 49cc, completely restored to original specification. **£450–500 BKS**

Yamaha quoted a power output of 4.8bhp at 7,000rpm for their FSIE (more commonly known as the 'Fizzy'), enough to attain almost 50mph and more than satisfy the average 16-year-old.

Zenith *(British 1904–50)*

1911 Zenith 8hp Gradua, side-valve, JAP V-twin engine, completely restored, Pioneer certificate, excellent condition. **£7,000–7,700 BKS**

For many years, the Zenith factory had as its trademark an early motorcycle behind bars with the word 'barred' diagonally across it. This referred to a period in the vintage and veteran days when Zenith was so overwhelmingly successful in hill climbs that many organisers banned Zenith riders from taking part. The reason for this level of success was the patented Gradua Gear which, contrary to common practice, allowed the rear wheel to move back and forth to compensate for the pulley adjustment, thus keeping belt tension constant. Moreover, this could be done on the move.

Dirt Bikes

1928 Douglas DT5 Speedway, 498cc, fore-and-aft flat-twin, 62.25 x 82mm bore and stroke.
£5,200–5,750 BKS

When speedway racing arrived in Britain from Australia during 1928, the new sport quickly caught the public's imagination, and before long almost all of the major UK manufacturers listed dirt-track models. Douglas was the first marque to establish dominance, largely due to the fact that the company's twins had benefited from a considerable amount of earlier development on the Australian long tracks.

1951 Norton 500T, 490cc, overhead-valve single.
£2,500–2,800 TEN

The 500T was introduced toward the end of 1948 and continued in production until 1954. Numerous works and privateer competition successes soon confirmed the Norton trials mount as a serious competitor. In fact, the legendary Geoff Duke rode one before he switched to road racing with the same company in 1949. This particular example was formerly the property of Norton works rider Dougie Connet.

1951 Royal Enfield Bullet Trials, 346cc, overhead-valve single, completely restored to original specification.
£5,800–6,500 BKS

Enfield revived the Bullet name in 1948 for a sensational new 350 sports bike with swinging-arm rear suspension. After the prototype's debut in the Colmore Cup trial, the Bullet went on to achieve its first major victory in the ISDT later that year. Although Royal Enfield's success in post-war trials owed much to the fact that the company was first in the field with swinging-arm suspension, it could be argued that works rider John Brittain, aided by the likes of Jack Stocker, Stan Holmes, Don Evans and younger brother Pat, made a greater contribution. In his book, *Classic British Trials Bikes*, Don Morley recounts that it was Enfield's practice to debut a works bike in ISDT form, then convert it for one-day trials. This machine began life as Billy Clark's mount in the 1951 ISDT, in which the factory team gained an FIM Gold Medal, and finished up as Pat Brittain's one-day machine. Later, it was used by Geoff Duke in the mid-1960s, and is pictured being ridden by the multi-World Champion in Ralph Venables' book, *British Trials Motorcycles: The Men and Their Machines*.

◄ 1956 Ariel HT3, 346cc, overhead-valve, single-cylinder engine, restored.
£3,500–4,000 BLM

Only 27 examples of the HT3 trials model were produced, far fewer than the more common 500 HT5. Thus, it is far more collectable, although it does not offer the performance of its larger brother.

1957 Matchless G3LC Trials, 348cc, overhead-valve single, 69 x 93mm bore and stroke, unrestored.
£900–1,000 H&H

Unlike today, when every form of motorcycle sport is very specialised, during the 1950s the same basic designs were often utilised for trials, scrambles and even road racing. The only differences were such components as camshafts, compression ratios and carburettor sizes.

▶ **1958 Triumph T20 Tiger Cub Trials,** 199cc, overhead-valve single, engine rebuilt, fitted with electronic ignition.
£1,500–1,800 BKS

The suitability of the Tiger Cub for trials competition was highlighted by its many excellent performances in the hands of works riders and privateers alike – men such as Roy Peplow, Gordon Farley, Johnny Giles and Ray Sayer, to name but four.

1959 BSA A10 Spitfire Scrambler, 646cc, overhead-valve, pre-unit twin, straight-through exhaust, completely restored.
£5,400–6,000 CStC

The Spitfire was sold in the USA as the Catalina Scrambler.

1961 Greeves MCS, 246cc, Villiers 34A 2-stroke single, straight-through exhaust system, alloy tank and mudguards, completely restored to concours condition.
£1,900–2,200 PC

This machine is the same as the model used by Dave Bickers to win the European championship.

1957 AJS Model 18CS, 497cc, overhead-valve single, 86 x 85.5mm bore and stroke, completely restored to concours condition.
£3,500–4,000 AMOC

Next to the BSA Gold Star, the AMC singles were probably the best of the big British heavyweight singles on the 1950s scrambles scene.

1960 Greeves 24TAS Scottish, 246cc, Villiers 32A 2-stroke, single-cylinder engine.
£1,000–1,200 BKS

Based in Thundersley, Essex, the small Greeves concern gained a fine reputation for sporting success in all forms of competition, but particularly trials and scrambles. The company had as its unorthodox technical trademarks a cast-aluminium beam front downtube and rubber-in-torsion, leading-link front forks. In its time, the 24TAS Scottish was the most popular of all British two-stroke trials bikes.

1962 Cotton Cougar, 246cc, Villiers piston-port, 2-stroke single, alloy head and barrel, leading-link front forks, swinging-arm rear suspension.
£1,600–1,800 COEC

The Cougar made use of a Parkinson square-barrel conversion to give the Villiers 36A engine more power.

1950 Triumph 5T Speed Twin, 499cc, overhead-valve, pre-unit twin, iron head and barrels.
£2,800–3,100 BKS

Introduced in 1937, the Speed Twin, with its vertical-twin engine, achieved rapid success and turned around Triumph's ailing fortunes. Renowned for its simplicity and lightness, the machine became the backbone of the company's post-war production, continuing in uprated guises until 1966.

▶ **1955 Triumph 5T Speed Twin,** 499cc, overhead-valve twin, 63 x 80mm bore and stroke, parcel rack on tank, headlamp nacelle, dualseat.
£4,000–4,500 VER

Nineteen-fifty-five was the first year that the Speed Twin featured a swinging-arm frame, replacing the sprung rear hub of the earliest machines. The swinging-arm 5T was built from 1955 to 1958, before being superseded by the new unit-construction model.

1951 Triumph Tiger 100, 499cc, overhead-valve, pre-unit twin, 4-speed foot-change gearbox, sprung hub, completely restored to concours condition.
£4,000–4,500 MAY

◀ **1960 Triumph T120 Bonneville,** 649cc, overhead-valve, pre-unit twin, splayed cylinder head, twin Amal Monobloc carburettors, completely restored to concours condition.
£5,800–6,500 PC

The original, early Bonneville, with its powder blue and silver finish, is without doubt a classic of its era; the later version never quite matched the beautiful style of the 1960/61 machine.

1961 Triumph T100A, 490cc, standard specification including 'bathtub' rear enclosure and valanced front mudguard.
£2,500–2,750 MAY

The T100A was only offered in 1960 and 1961, being replaced for the 1962 season by the more sporting T100SS.

► **1966 Triumph T100SS,** 490cc, overhead-valve, unit twin-cylinder engine, 69 x 65.5mm bore and stroke, original specification, restored, excellent condition. **£2,000–2,500 MAY**

With its sporty appearance and compact build, the T100SS was one of the most popular British bikes of its time. It continued in production until 1970, receiving the frame of the high-performance T100T model in 1967.

◄ **1967 Triumph T100SS,** 490cc, overhead-valve, unit twin, Amal 376 1in carburettor, standard specification. **£2,400–2,650 BKS**

The T100SS was the single-carburettor sports model of the Triumph 500 unit family. It was offered between 1962 and 1970, early versions having a 'half-bathtub' rear enclosure, which was dropped after the 1965 model year.

1963 Triumph TR6SS, 650cc, overhead-valve, unit twin, single-downtube frame.
£3,600–4,500 BLM

1964 Triumph Cub, 199cc, recently restored.
£1,250–1,400 DSCM

◄ **1967 Triumph T20B Bantam Cub,** 199cc, overhead-valve, unit-construction, single-cylinder engine, completely restored, excellent condition throughout. **£1,600–2,000 TCTR**

The Bantam Cub first appeared for the 1966 season, being based on a BSA frame, forks and other cycle parts.

◀ **1971 Triumph Trophy 650,** 649cc, overhead-valve, unit-construction, twin-cylinder engine, US-specification machine.
£2,600–2,900 OXM

The Trophy 650 was essentially a single-carburettor version of the T120 Bonneville. Many riders preferred it to the latter, because it was easier to ride and easier to maintain.

▶ **1975 Triumph Trident T160,** 750cc, restored, excellent condition.
£3,300–3,650 BKS

By the early 1970s, the need to update the Trident was considered essential if it was to continue to be a force in the superbike market. Certain features were deemed necessary for the NVT group's flagship model, namely disc brakes and electric starting. The latter resulted in the adoption of a new frame and the inclined cylinder block previously utilised on the Rocket Three to accommodate the battery and starter.

◀ **1961 Velocette Venom,** 499cc, overhead-valve, pre-unit single, converted to Thruxton-type specification, swept-back exhaust pipe, twin-leading-shoe front brake, heat guard, oil tank, rev-counter, racing-type seat, excellent condition.
£4,000–5,000 MAY

For many, the Venom was the ultimate single-cylinder machine, with its excellent combination of speed and handling.

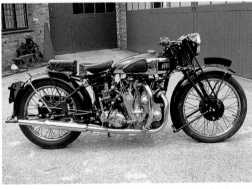

1939 Vincent-HRD Series A, 1000cc, overhead-valve V-twin, siamesed exhaust, dual front brakes, sprung saddle, pillion pad.
£33,500–37,500 VER

1955 Vincent-HRD Black Prince, 1000cc, overhead-valve V-twin, siamesed exhaust, fully-enclosed bodywork, dualseat, excellent condition.
£14,800–16,500 VER

1963 Triumph Tiger Cub Trials, 200cc, overhead-valve single, recently rebuilt, engine overhauled, electronic ignition, new chains and sprockets, cycle parts refurbished or replaced as necessary, complies with current Pre-'65 Trials regulations, in need of running in.
£1,600–1,800 BKS

1963 Dot Roger Kyyfin Replica Scrambler, 500cc, overhead-valve twin, alloy fuel tank, restored, excellent condition.
£4,500–5,000 DOT

1965 Jawa Two-Valve Speedway Bike, 499cc, overhead-valve engine, total-loss oil system, alloy tank, ex-Peter Collins.
£2,500–2,750 JCZ

1968 BSA BB4 Grand Prix Scrambler, 441cc, overhead-valve single.
£4,000–5,000 BOC

◄ **1960 Moto Guzzi Three-Wheeler,** 754cc, 90° V-twin, 80 x 74mm bore and stroke, ex-Italian Army.
£1,600–2,000 MAY

This military Moto Guzzi can be fitted with tank tracks for use on rough terrain. The engine was the forerunner of the unit fitted to the company's series of V-twin motorcycles.

► **1972 Norton 750 Commando Interpol,** overhead-valve, pre-unit twin, disc front brake, completely restored to full police specification, including radio equipment, panniers and fairing, original apart from early Interstate exhaust pipes.
£4,000–4,800 PC

This machine was supplied new to the Lancashire Constabulary. At that time, the choice for British police forces was either the Interpol or Triumph's Saint.

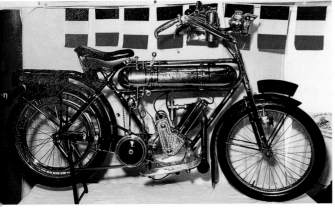

◀ **1912 Magat Debon Model A,** 397cc, overhead-valve, inclined single, 2-speed hand-change gearbox, belt final drive, copper fuel tank, tyre-drive klaxon horn, concours condition. **£20,000+ ATD**

This 'over-the-counter' racing motorcycle was built in Grenoble and is probably the only surviving example – certainly in this condition.

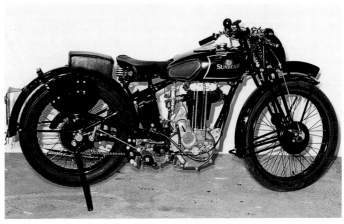

▶ **1932 Sunbeam TT Model,** 493cc, overhead-valve, single-port single. **£4,800–5,300 BKS**

The year 1932 saw Sunbeam entering the TT on a private basis, although still with considerable factory support behind the scenes. For that year, the Model 90, with its two-valve engine, featured an improved lubrication system, enclosed valve gear and a four-speed, foot-change gearbox.

◀ **1953 MV Agusta Competizione,** 124cc, overhead-camshaft, single-cylinder engine, concours condition. **£12,000–15,000 MVA**

In the smaller-capacity classes, MV offered its paying customers pushrod, rather than overhead-cam, engines, with the exception of the pure racing Competizione model.

1957 MV Agusta 500GP Four, 497.5cc, double-overhead-camshaft, 4-cylinder engine, 53 x 56.4mm bore and stroke, 4 Dell'Orto SS28 carburettors, 5-speed close-ratio gearbox. **£75,000+ PC**

This works MV Four is of the type raced by Surtees, Hartle, Hocking and Hailwood during the golden era of GP racing in the late 1950s and early 1960s.

1961 Moto Morini Corsarino Competizione, 49cc, overhead-valve, unit single, 4-speed gearbox.
£1,700–1,900 INM

One of the few four-stroke-engined machines to race in the 50cc class outside factory level, the Corsarino Competizione was an 'over-the-counter' racer available to the general public.

1969 Rickman Metisse Triumph, 749cc, overhead-valve, unit twin, close-ratio gear cluster, front and rear disc brakes, magnesium hubs, Morgo 750cc conversion with central-plug cylinder head, updated for Classic racing events with Beyer Bransden electronic ignition and belt primary drive, ex-Percy Tait.
£3,400–3,800 BKS

◀ **1975 Harley-Davidson RR350,** 349cc, piston-port, 2-stroke parallel twin, dual-disc front and drum rear brakes, 18in wheels.
£3,400–3,750 BKS

The RR350 was a development of the works machine campaigned by the late Renzo Pasolini in the early 1970s. This particular bike is a semi-works production model, believed to have won the 1975 Italian National Racing Championship.

▶ **1977 Fantic GP50,** 49cc, Minerelli piston-port, 2-stroke single, 41 x 37.7mm bore and stroke, 6-speed gearbox, 5-spoke Campagnolo wheels, disc front brake.
£2,500–3,000 RFC

Fantic was known primarily for its off-road models, but this tarmac racer proves that the company could make other models, too.

◀ **1982 Kawasaki KR250,** 249cc, disc-valve, 2-stroke, inline twin, 6-speed gearbox, disc brakes front and rear, single-shock rear suspension, ex-J. P. Balde works machine.
£13,500–15,000 SGR

During the late 1970s and early 1980s, Kawasaki gained a whole clutch of world-championship titles, using two-stroke inline twins.

953 Lambretta LD125, 124cc, standard specification
part from pillion saddle and rear carrier.
800–950 MAY

**This model has a side-flap for access to the tickler
on the carburettor.**

1957 Lambretta Model D, 148cc, air-cooled, 2-stroke
single, 57 x 58mm bore and stroke, 6bhp at 4,750rpm,
original and unrestored.
£560–700 MAY

964 Lambretta SX150, 149cc, carrier, spare wheel,
nrestored, original specification.
700–800 MAY

**The SX150 was one of Lambretta's 'Slimline' series
of scooters.**

1911 Bradbury and Sidecar, 550cc, inlet-over-exhaust
single, forward-mounted magneto, belt drive,
acetylene lighting.
£8,000–9,000 VER

◄ **1957 Triton Special,** 649cc,
pre-unit T110 engine, twin
carburettors, swept-back exhaust,
Daytona megaphone silencers, AMC
gearbox, wideline frame, racing tank
and seat, half-fairing, alloy rims.
£2,000–2,500 MAY

**The basis of the Triton was a
Triumph engine and Norton
Featherbed frame. Most were
built as either café racers or
competition mounts.**

► **c1963 Norton
Domiracer,** 650cc,
overhead-valve
Dominator engine,
AMC-type gearbox,
four-leading-shoe front
brake, conical rear hub,
Manx-pattern bodywork.
£3,000–3,300 JMR

**This machine was built
from a variety of models
of differing ages.**

◀ **c1964 Com-Dom Special,** 499cc, overhead-valve Vincent Comet engine, 84 x 90mm bore and stroke.
£2,500–3,000 BMR

The 'Com-Dom' name comes from the combination of a Vincent Comet single-cylinder engine with a Norton Dominator wideline frame, Norton gearbox and twin-leading-shoe front brake conversion.

▶ **1990s Egli Vincent,** 998cc, 1955 overhead-valve, Vincent V-twin engine, Egli oil-in-frame chassis, 1970s Triumph front disc brake.
£10,000+ JMR

Switzerland's Fritz Egli began building specials powered by the British Vincent engine during the late 1960s, both as complete machines and frame kits for customers to fit their own engines.

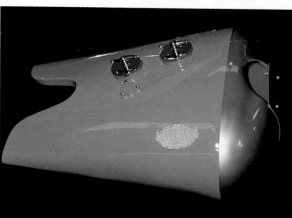

◀ An AJW tank, with separate sections for fuel and oil, completely restored and refinished in original colour scheme for 500cc JAP-engined machine, 1927.
£450–500 ETE

A Grasshopper Motorcycle Club Chingford enamelled white metal badge, 1950s, 2 x 2¾in (5 x 7cm).
£30–35 ATF

A Velocette Motor Cycles brochure, 1930, 10 x 7½in (25.5 x 19cm).
£22–25 DM

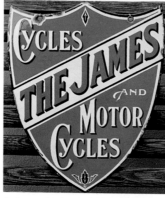

A James Cycles and Motor Cycles enamel sign, 1930s, 22in (56cm) high.
£270–300 MSMP

A New Hudson enamel sign, 1912, 12 x 18in (30.5 x 45.5cm).
£750–850 BRUM

c1962 Triumph T20 Tiger Cub Trials Replica,
199cc, overhead-valve, unit single, Amal Concentric
Mk 1 carburettor, alloy mudguards, fork gaiters,
unrestored, unused for 5 years.
£650–750 PS

This machine was built from spare parts to create
a replica of the successful Cub Trials model.

1964 BSA C15 Trials Replica, 247cc, overhead-valve
single, alloy mudguards, oil and fuel tanks, silencer
and wheel rims, converted to C15T specification,
but with changes to lower weight.
£900–1,000 MAY

c1967 Jawa Two-Valve Speedway, 499cc, 2-valve,
overhead-valve single, Dell'Orto SS1 carburettor,
3-spring clutch, single-sided rear hub, standard
specification apart from ex-works ice racing head and
Lucas SR-type magneto in place of original Pal type
(standard head supplied with machine).
£1,200–1,350 BKS

The first owner of this machine was Martin Ashby,
who had the frame plated and used it for a short while
before returning to a JAP. Subsequently, he sold the
bike to Norman Parker, team manager at Swindon.
Norman, brother of Jack Parker and a top pre-war
speedway star, had Bob Jones, the Swindon Speedway
mechanic, prepare and maintain it for his son, John.
Unfortunately, John never made it in speedway like his
father and uncle, but used the machine for practice
and minor races for about six years. Then it passed
to Fred Bridewell of Devizes, whose two sons rode it
in speedway and grasstrack events; it also featured
in the novice careers of several top Swindon riders.
Since 1984, it has been used for classic speedway in
the UK and abroad. The late 'wild man' Vic Lonsdale
won the Jubilee Classic Race at Exeter in 1989 on
this machine, and speedway fans have seen it in
action at Swindon, Reading, Peterborough, Exeter,
Long Eaton, Sheffield, Oxford and many other tracks.

1963 Dot Demon, 246cc, Villiers 2-stroke single,
square barrel and head, alloy tank and mudguards,
concours condition.
£1,200–1,500 DOT

The Demon was typical of British two-stroke
scramblers of the era. Similar machines were made
by Greeves, Cotton and James.

1964 Cotton Cobra, 247cc, Villiers Starmaker
2-stroke, single-cylinder engine.
£1,800–2,000 COEC

Villiers introduced its new Starmaker engine at the
1962 Earl's Court show. Its high performance made
it the first choice for several specialist competition
builders, including Greeves, Cotton and DMW.

1967 Dot Demon Mk 5, 360cc, 2-stroke single, alloy head
and barrel, Amal Concentric Mk 1 carburettor, Albion
gearbox, completely restored to concours condition.
£1,800–2,000 DOT

1973 Cotton Enduro, 170cc, Minerelli piston-port,
unit-construction single, wide-ratio foot-change gearbox.
£1,000–1,250 COEC

Today, the Cotton Enduro is a very rare machine.

◄ **1971 Greeves Pathfinder,** 169cc, 2-stroke, single-cylinder engine, 20bhp at 8,000rpm, 6-speed gearbox, unrestored.
£550–650 PS

Like many other small British motorcycle manufacturers, Greeves suffered when Villiers stopped supplying its two-stroke engines. This forced the company to look elsewhere, and eventually it chose the Austrian Puch engine to power its new Pathfinder trials model. Bert Greeves himself debuted the Pathfinder prototype at the Greybeard Trial toward the end of 1969.

c1970 Montesa Cota Trials, 123cc, 54 x 54mm bore and stroke, 13bhp at 7,000rpm.
£650–800 PC

Montesa trials bikes were marketed with considerable success in the UK by Jim Sandford.

1973 Dot Minerelli Trials, 174cc, piston-port, 2-stroke single, Dell'Orto VHB square-slide carburettor.
£1,200–1,500 DOT

This model combined British cycle parts with an Italian engine.

► **1975 Bultaco T350 Sherpa,** 326cc, piston-port, 2-stroke, single-cylinder engine, 83.2 x 60mm bore and stroke, 9:1 compression ratio, 21bhp at 5,000rpm, unrestored, in need of attention.
£250–300 BLM

The production version of the 350T (as opposed to the original Comerford conversion) arrived in October 1972.

1979 CCM Enduro, 499cc, overhead-valve single, Marzocchi forks, alloy tank, nickel-plated frame, fewer than 1,000 miles from new.
£3,200–3,600 H&H

Alan Clews was the man behind the Bolton based CCM marque. Like the majority of his models, the Enduro was powered by a development of the BSA Victor engine.

1979 Suzuki RM100, 98cc, 2-stroke single, leading-axle long-travel forks, twin-shock rear suspension, original specification, unrestored.
£300–350 PS

The RM100 was a favourite bike in schoolboy motocross events during the late 1970s and early 1980s.

Military Motorcycles

◀ **1941 Indian 741B,** 500cc, side-valve V-twin.
£5,500–6,100 BKS

Development of a new 500-class side-valve V-twin for military use began at Indian's Springfield factory during 1939. The resultant machine, the 741B, was adopted in relatively small numbers by the American military, but was used extensively by British and Commonwealth forces on all fronts during WWII.

> A known continuous history can add value to and enhance the enjoyment of a motorcycle.

▶ **1941 Indian 741B,** 500cc, side-valve V-twin.
£5,500–6,100 BKS

This machine was used during the making of the feature film *A Bridge Too Far*, the account of the Allied airborne assault on Arnhem during 1944.

1941 Indian 741B, 500cc, side-valve, V-twin engine, original military specification, unrestored.
£10,000–12,000 PC

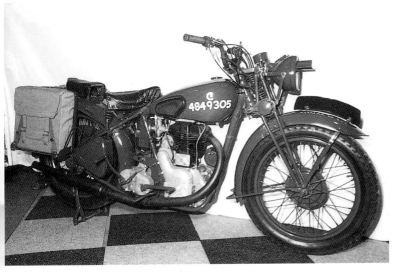

◀ **1942 Royal Enfield WD COB,** overhead-valve, single-cylinder engine, 4-speed foot-change gearbox, girder forks, rigid frame, original canvas saddlebags, ex-RAF.
£1,800–2,000 BMC

The 'B' in the model suffix indicates that the machine is fitted with a Burman gearbox. This model was made for a few months only in 1942 and 1943. As a result, it is very rare; particularly when compared to other military motorcycles of the same era.

1942 Harley-Davidson WLA, 742cc, side-valve, V-twin engine, 69.85 x 96.83mm bore and stroke, 23bhp at 4,600rpm, 3-speed hand-change gearbox, chain final drive, completely restored.
£4,000–4,500 PC

Auction prices

Miller's only includes motorcycles declared sold. Our guide prices take into account the buyer's premium, VAT on the premium, and the extent of any published catalogue information relating to condition and provenance. To identify motorcycles sold at auction, cross-refer the source code at the end of each caption with the Key to Illustrations on page 167.

▶ **1945 BSA M20,** 496cc, side-valve single, 82 x 94mm bore and stroke, foot-change gearbox.
£1,800–2,000 MVT

1945 Royal Enfield Model CO, 346cc, overhead-valve, single-cylinder engine, 70 x 90mm bore and stroke, magneto ignition, 4-speed foot-change gearbox.
£1,600–1,800 BLM

1956 Triumph TRW, 496cc, side-valve, twin-cylinder engine, non-original handlebars, ex-RAF machine.
£1,700–2,000 AT

The TRW was used by the RAF for escort, police and general despatch work.

◄ 1960 Moto Guzzi 3x3, 754cc, air-cooled, overhead-valve, 90° V-twin engine, 6-speed gearbox, including reverse, drive transmitted to all 3 wheels, ex-Italian Army.
£1,600–1,800 BKS

This machine was produced between 1960 and 1963, being designed for use by the Italian Army's Alpine Corps. The engine was the forerunner of the famous V-twin that powered many Moto Guzzi motorcycles.

▶ 1961 Triumph TRW, 496cc, side-valve twin, siamesed exhaust, 4-speed foot-change gearbox, telescopic forks, rigid frame, correct canvas saddlebags, tank-top grid, repainted olive green, ex-RAF.
£1,700–1,950 CotC

The TRW saw widespread use with the Royal Air Force from the 1950s until it was finally retired in the 1970s.

◄ 1974 Condor Militaire, 340cc, bevel-driven overhead-camshaft, unit-construction, Ducati widecase single, 5-speed gearbox, Condor-built duplex frame, Marzocchi forks, large full-width Grimeca drum brakes, Bosch headlamp, carrier, panniers, ex-Swiss Army.
£1,200–1,350 TGA

The Condor marque had a long history of supplying motorcycles to the Swiss armed forces.

Monkey Bikes

1968 Benelli Monkey Bike, 48cc, 2-stroke, horizontal single, single-speed automatic transmission.
£900–1,100 SGR

This machine was designed to fold away into the boot of a car.

1978 Honda ST70, 72cc, overhead-camshaft, horizontal single, 47 x 41.4mm bore and stroke, high-level exhaust, bolted-up wheels, dualseat, pillion footrests.
£550–650 CARS

1972 Honda Z50A, 49cc, overhead-camshaft, horizontal single-cylinder engine, 41 x 49.5mm bore and stroke, 2.5bhp at 6,000rpm.
£1,000–1,200 VICO

▶ **1979 Honda Dax,** 71.8cc, overhead-camshaft, horizontal single-cylinder engine, completely restored to concours condition.
£700–770 H&H

The Dax was a development of the earlier ST70. Both machines were larger versions of the original Monkey Bike concept.

Mopeds

1956 Norman Nippy, 49cc, 2-stroke single, alloy head and iron barrel, leading-link forks.
£90–100 MAY

The Nippy made use of the German Sachs engine.

1964 Laverda Laverdino, 47.8cc, 2-stroke, single-cylinder engine, 1.5bhp at 4,200rpm.
£400–500 ILO

The Laverdino was unusual in having cable-operated front and rear disc brakes. Some 5,000 were built.

1968 Velo Solex, 30cc, 2-stroke, single-cylinder engine mounted above front wheel.
£200–240 PC

1969 Vespa Ciao, 49cc, horizontal 2-stroke single, in need of restoration.
£40–50 MAY

◄ **1970 Ariel 3,** 49cc, 3-wheel trike-type moped.
£180–200 PM

With an engine made by the Dutch Anker concern, the Ariel 3 proved a major sales flop. Abortive designs such as this did much to hasten the BSA Group's demise. The BSA computer was still ordering components such as engines and tyres long after it should have stopped, resulting in vast stocks of unsaleable items.

► **1972 Puch MS50D,**
49cc, fan-cooled, 2-stroke, single-cylinder engine, 3-speed twistgrip gear-change, swinging-arm rear suspension, pressed-steel frame, original and unrestored.
£200–220 PS

Several hundred of the MS50D model were purchased by the British Royal Mail.

Police Bikes

◀ **1951 Triumph 5T Speed Twin,** 499cc, pre-unit parallel twin, sprung hub, pillion pad, Avon fairing.
£2,500–2,750 RFC

The Speed Twin saw widespread use with police forces during the years immediately after WWII. This machine was purchased new by the Metropolitan Police in May 1951.

1980 Moto Guzzi 850T3 Police, 844cc, overhead-valve, 90° V-twin engine, 5-speed gearbox, shaft final drive, fairing, horns, panniers.
£1,000–1,150 IVC

Miller's is a price GUIDE not a price LIST

1982 Kawasaki KZ1000, 998cc, double-overhead-camshaft, across-the-frame four, 5-speed gearbox, triple disc brakes, cast alloy wheels, front and rear crashbars, panniers, fairing, ex-US police.
£1,400–1,550 H&H

1983 Kawasaki KZ1000, 998cc, double-overhead-camshaft four, imported from USA in 1997.
£1,800–2,000 BKS

The KZ1000 was the first police model to comfortably exceed 130mph. This particular machine saw service with the San Diego Police Department on highway patrol duties.

Racing Bikes

1928 Sunbeam TT Model 90, 493cc, overhead-valve, single-cylinder engine, 3-speed gearbox, restored.
£6,500–£7,200 BKS

In June 1928, Charlie Dodson won a famous victory in the Senior TT in dreadfully wet conditions. His mount was an overhead-valve Sunbeam single, the TT Model 90, the engine of which had been developed by George Dance. The machine was nicknamed 'Bullnose' due to the front curve of its flat tank.

▶ **1931 Velocette KTT,** 348cc, overhead-camshaft, vertical single-cylinder engine.
£5,500–6,100 BKS

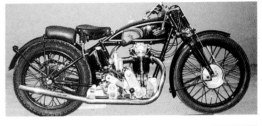

c1931 Douglas Sprint Special Replica, 499cc, overhead-valve, fore-and-aft twin-cylinder engine, 3-speed hand-change gearbox, built 1995 from original and new components costing £3,000.
£5,500–6,100 BKS

▶ **1932 Rudge Sprinter,** 350cc, 4-valve, twin-port single.
£3,000–3,500 REC

1932 Sunbeam Model 90, 498cc, overhead-valve, single-cylinder engine, 4-speed gearbox, restored.
£5,500–6,100 BKS

By the mid-1920s, George Dance's development programme had moulded the overhead-valve Sunbeam into one of the most formidable racing motorcycles of the vintage era, the 500cc Model 90 in particular being a match for anything in its class by the decade's end. Despite the wholesale failure of the works 350s in the 1928 Isle of Man Junior TT, Sunbeam came good in the Senior event, Charles Dodson winning an eventful race after crashing and remounting, while seventh and 15th places for team-mates Francesco Franconi and Luigi Arcangeli gained the Wolverhampton marque the Team Prize. Dodson triumphed again in the Senior in 1929, which was an outstanding year for Sunbeam, with wins at the French, German, Austrian, and Italian Grands Prix.

1936 NSU 501SS, 494cc, overhead-camshaft single, 80 x 99mm bore and stroke, 30bhp at 6,000rpm.
£8,500–9,400 BKS

NSU was set up in 1873, and by 1901 had entered motorcycle production at Neckarsulm; in fact, the name of the company was formed from three letters of the town's name. By 1910, the marque had become so successful that it ranked second to Indian as the most popular imported make sold in Britain. Former Norton engineer Walter Moore made a significant contribution to NSU's success during the 1930s. He had designed the British company's CSI overhead-camshaft engine that won the Senior TT on its first appearance in 1927. However, he felt that the company showed a lack of commitment to further development of his engine, so he left to join NSU in 1910 and would remain there until just before the onset of WWII. As a result, by 1931, NSU was able to field an overhead-camshaft racer at the TT. Most importantly, by 1935, the company was leading on the race tracks with a developed overhead-camshaft racer ridden by the formidable Briton Tommy Bullus.

1936 Excelsior ER12 Manxman, 349cc, overhead-camshaft, 4-stroke single, 75 x 79mm bore and stroke, dry-sump lubrication, 4-speed foot-change gearbox.
£4,500–5,000 H&H

The Manxman was sold in both sports and racing forms; its first year of production was 1935.

1938 Excelsior GRII Manxman, 249cc, bevel-driven, overhead-camshaft single, 67 x 70.65mm bore and stroke, 4-speed foot-change gearbox.
£4,300–4,800 H&H

◀ **1936 Terrot T Works Racer HCP 350,** 349cc, overhead-valve, single-cylinder engine, 74 x 80mm bore and stroke, 4-speed foot-change gearbox, outrigger support bearing, girder forks, plunger rear suspension.
£8,000–10,000 TDD

For many years, Terrot was one of the major French racing marques and it enjoyed a string of track successes.

1939 Norton, 490cc, bevel-driven, overhead-camshaft, single-cylinder engine, 4-speed foot-change gearbox, alloy fuel and oil tanks, restored, excellent condition.
£8,000–10,000 **VER**

1948 Triumph Grand Prix, 499cc, overhead-valve, parallel twin, alloy head and barrel.
£4,800–£5,700 **BKS**

The very first post-WWII Manx Grand Prix was won in 1946 by Ernie Lyons on a Triumph Tiger 100. This had a silicone-aluminium cylinder head and barrel adapted from a wartime generator designed to charge the batteries of RAF bombers in flight. Along with other competition extras, the machine had an unusual rear suspension system developed by Edward Turner, the springs being contained within an oversize wheel hub, thereafter known as a sprung hub. Subsequently developed and named the Grand Prix, the new Triumph racer became a team entry for the 1948 Senior TT, but all failed for a variety of reasons. In all, 175 of these machines were sold, and it is thought that a further 20 engines were built.

1948 AJS 7R, 348cc, 74 x 81mm bore and stroke, magnesium outer engine covers.
£8,000–8,800 **BKS**

Introduced in 1948, the 7R featured a single-overhead-camshaft engine which, while entirely new, drew heavily on experience gained by AJS during the pre-war years with their 'cammy' singles. The new model fulfilled two roles, providing privateers with a competitive mount and enabling AJS to run a works team in the 350cc Grand Prix alongside the 500cc 'Porcupine' works twin. The model remained in production until 1963, being developed continuously to keep it to the fore in competition.

> A known continuous history can add value to and enhance the enjoyment of a motorcycle.

► **1949 Triumph Grand Prix**, 499cc, overhead-valve twin, 4-speed close-ratio gearbox, sprung-hub rear suspension, telescopic front forks, completely restored to concours condition.
£10,500–12,000 **BKS**

A notable feature of the Grand Prix model was its Turner-designed sprung-hub rear suspension system.

c1950s Excelsior Manxman Special, 249cc, overhead-camshaft, Manxman single-cylinder engine, Amal TT carburettor, duplex frame, telescopic forks, swinging-arm rear suspension, alloy tanks, rims and mudguards, restored.
£5,000–5,500 H&H

Due to the reluctance of the major British manufacturers to produce over-the-counter 250cc racing machines during the post-WWII period, it was left to the special builders to meet this need – often using more modern cycle parts with pre-war engines. This machine is just such a special.

1954 AJS E95 Porcupine, 497cc, quantity of spares including a 'sprint' tank needed for making adjustments to the engine while running, ex-works and Tom Arter.
£158,000+ BKS

While the Norton is Britain's most successful post-WWII Grand Prix racing motorcycle, this country's first success in the modern era's World Championships was achieved by AJS. And the machine that carried Les Graham to his, and AJS', first and only World Championship in 1949 was the legendary Porcupine. Originally, the Porcupine had been designed with forced induction in mind – supercharged multi-cylinder engines had begun to threaten the single's supremacy toward the end of the 1930s – but when the FIM banned supercharging at the end of 1946, the design was too far advanced to be altered substantially, although the cylinder heads were revised to raise the compression ratio. Typed E90, but dubbed 'Porcupine' because of its distinctive spiked head finning, AJS' new challenger debuted at the 1947 Isle of Man TT in the hands of Les Graham and Jock West, the pair finishing 9th and 14th respectively after a variety of problems. Carburetion had been the Porcupine's biggest fault, and over the years a bewildering number of different induction arrangements were tried. The bike was also bedevilled by magneto shaft failure, which would not be solved until chain drive for the magneto was adopted on the revised E95 engine. Introduced in 1952, the latter had its cylinders tilted up at 45 degrees, requiring a new frame, and featured a pressed-up crankshaft with one-piece conrods and roller big-ends in place of the E90's one-piece crank and shell-type bearings. For 1954, the E95 Porcupine gained a pannier-style fuel tank that extended down on each side of the engine, thus lowering the centre of gravity and affording a degree of streamlining. The downside was the need for a pump to raise fuel to the carburettors, and a complicated delivery system that required the mechanics to stand the bike on its rear wheel to prime the header tank for starting. Bob McIntyre, Derek Farrant and Rod Coleman were the riders that year, the last providing the Porcupine with its best international results of the season, placing second in Ulster and winning the Swedish Grand Prix. Sadly, AJS withdrew from direct involvement in racing at the season's end. Only four complete E90 and four E95 machines were built, plus a number of spare engines. With the exception of this machine, they were raced only by the works team. This E95 was acquired by Tom Arter in 1963 from the AMC race-shop. By then, however, even his development skills could not restore its competitiveness, although progress was made in simplifying the fuel system, increasing maximum power and improving the handling by fitting Girling rear dampers and G50 front forks. The scale of modifications deemed necessary, however, forced the project's abandonment. Subsequently, the machine appeared in classic events during the 1980s.

1954 Norton Manx 30M, 499cc, overhead-camshaft, single-cylinder engine, restored, fitted with 1953-pattern Featherbed frame, period cycle parts.
£9,800–10,800 **BKS**

The most famous single-cylinder racers of all time were produced by Norton. 'Functional Harmonisation' was a term invented by Joe Craig to epitomise everything he believed about the camshaft engine. Few riders were able to race the Manx Norton to its absolute limit, and while the engine could only be improved slowly by the factory, there were independent engineers who could breathe extra life into it. By 1950, the new Featherbed Manx began to make an appearance, and this took the machines to the absolute peak of their achievements. The engine of this machine was delivered new in May 1955, the receiving agent being listed as Daniels/Surtees.

◀ **1955 NSU Sportmax,** 247cc, overhead-camshaft single, dry clutch, close-ratio gearbox, leading-link front forks, aluminium tank and seat base.
£8,000–9,000 PC

The Sportmax was a limited-production racing motorcycle. In the hands of H. P. 'Happy' Müller, it won the 1955 250cc World Championship title. It was also raced by the likes of John Surtees and Mike Hailwood.

▶ **1955 Matchless G45,** 498cc, overhead-valve, twin-cylinder engine, 66 x 72.8mm bore and stroke, short-megaphone exhausts, 19in wheels, 'jampot' rear suspension units, engine rebuilt 1979, only 30 miles covered since, unused for past 12 years.
£20,000–22,000 BKS

The G45 was built between 1953 and 1957, and had an engine based on the G9 roadster unit. This machine was originally campaigned by Frank Perris while sponsored by the Arter brothers. He rode it in the 1955 Senior TT.

◄ **1955 Norton Manx 30M,** 499cc, double-overhead-camshaft single, 4-speed close-ratio gearbox, twin-leading-shoe front brake, original specification, letter of authenticity signed by John Surtees.
£14,800–16,300 BKS

This particular machine was purchased in 1955 by Sammy Miller as a 348cc Manx 40M. Subsequently, it was sold to John Surtees, and later to another rider who had a 500 engine fitted by leading Norton tuner Phil Kettle.

1956 AJS 7R, 348cc chain-driven, overhead-camshaft single, 4-speed gearbox, dry clutch, restored to original specification 1985/86.
£13,600–15,000 BKS

This machine was judged Best Racing Motorcycle at Manchester's Classic Bike Show in 1986. Since then, it has only been used for one lap of the TT course during a parade and two 15 minute test sessions at Bruntingthorpe.

AJS – The Boy Racer

Built from 1948 to 1963, Associated Motor Cycles' AJS 7R, known as 'The Boy Racer', was one of the most successful 'over-the-counter' racing motorcycles of all time. While, initially, not as powerful as the Velocette KTT and 350 Manx Norton, the 7R's robust and simple construction endeared it to privateers responsible for their own maintenance. The duplex loop frame and teledraulic front forks remained essentially unchanged throughout production, but the engine underwent almost continuous revision: the valve angle was narrowed progressively, the crankshaft was made stronger and, in 1956, the engine dimensions were changed from the original long-stroke 74 x 90mm to squarer 75.5 x 78mm. AMC's own gearbox replaced the previous Burman-made assembly for the 1958 season, while engine development continued almost to the end of production, by which time the 7R was putting out around 41bhp.

1956 MV Agusta 175 CSS, 172.4cc, overhead-camshaft, unit-construction single, 59.5 x 62mm bore and stroke, magneto ignition, 5-speed gearbox, Earles forks, limited-production 'over-the-counter' racer.
£10,000–11,000 PC

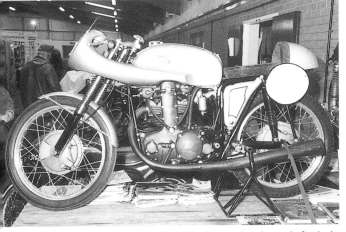

1956 Parilla Biaberro, 175cc, gear-driven, double-overhead-camshaft, single-cylinder engine, hairpin valve springs, magneto mounted in front of crankcase, 5-speed gearbox, aluminium fairing/tank, oil tank and rims, full-width hubs, sole example built.
£25,000–30,000 SGR

'Biaberro' means twin-camshaft.

► **1961 AJS 7R,** 348cc, chain-driven, overhead-camshaft, single-cylinder engine, 4-speed AMC gearbox, dry clutch, standard specification.
£11,900–13,100 BKS

This machine was formerly owned by the legendary AJS and Matchless specialists, the Arter brothers, who acted as development testers for the Plumstead factory. Included in Tom Arter's race team were the likes of Hugh Anderson and Mike Duff. This bike was last raced (still under the Arter banner) in the Isle of Man TT in 1984, ridden by Dave Hughes, but at that time with a 496cc Matchless G50 engine installed.

1962 BSA C15 Clubman's Racer, 247cc, overhead-valve, unit single, tuned engine, high-level exhaust, alloy wheel rims, flyscreen, racing seat and front mudguard.
£700–800 CStC

This machine was built from a standard C15 roadster.

► **c1960 BSA Bantam Racer,** 123cc, piston-port, 2-stroke single, tuned engine, high-level expansion-chamber exhaust, Yamaha forks and front wheel, alloy rims, racing tank, seat and fairing, rev-counter.
£1,800–2,100 BKS

1966 Cotton Telstar Mk 2, 247cc, Villiers Starmaker 2-stroke, single-cylinder engine, 4-speed close-ratio gearbox.
£2,800–3,200 COEC

The Telstar competed with the Greeves Silverstone and DMW Hornet in the two-stroke, clubman's, 'over-the-counter' racer sales war of the mid-1960s.

1967 Ducati Monza, 248cc, bevel-driven, overhead-camshaft single, 5-speed gearbox, wet clutch, engine rebuilt to full Mach 1 specification 1998, 32mm Amal Concentric Mk 1 carburettor, Japanese full-width alloy hubs, braced swinging arm with extended pivot, Vic Camp-type tank, Yamaha TR2 seat.
£600–700 BKS

1970 Honda CB450 Special, 498cc, double-overhead-camshaft, parallel twin-cylinder engine, four-leading-shoe front brake, twin-leading-shoe rear brake, finished in works Honda colours.
£2,600–3,000 BKS

The engine of this machine is basically a CB450 converted to full 500 specification.

1969/70 Guazzoni Cadet 60, 60cc, air-cooled, disc-valve single, 45 x 37.5mm bore and stroke, rear-facing exhaust, sand-cast crankcases, 6-speed gearbox, Ceriani racing forks, limited production.
£2,500–3,000 PC

This machine was designed specifically for use in the Italian national hill climb championships, which it won in 1969.

1960 AJS 7R Surtees Special, 348cc, special flywheels, magneto/coil ignition, Manx Norton gearbox containing 6-speed Schafleitner cluster, Rickman disc front brake, Manx rear hub, 19in alloy wheel rims.
£9,500–£10,500 BKS

This machine, Tom Arter's first special-framed AMC race bike, features a frame designed by John Surtees and built by Ken Sprayson of Reynolds Tubes. It had been Surtees' intention to create a competitive machine for British short-circuit events, but objections from his boss at MV, Count Agusta, plus increasing car-racing commitments meant that he never raced the bike, which passed to Rex Butcher and thence to Tom Arter.

1970 Seeley G50, 496cc, chain-driven, overhead-camshaft, single-cylinder engine.
£23,000–25,500 BKS

Colin Seeley took over the AMC race department during 1965/66. This particular machine was supplied to former GP star Tommy Robb, who rode it to fourth place in the 1970 500 World Championship.

1976 MV Agusta Magni 750 Special, 750cc, double-overhead-camshaft, 4-cylinder engine, 1-piece cylinder, Magni exhaust, 5-speed gearbox, chain-drive conversion, cast alloy wheels.
£14,500–16,000 COYS

This particular machine was built by ex-MV Agusta race mechanic and later team manager Arturo Magni for an Italian endurance racing team.

1974 Triumph 'Penetration' Sprint Bike, 820cc, overhead-valve, pre-unit, vertical twin, supercharged, front and rear disc brakes, alloy fuel and oil tanks.
£4,800–5,500 BKS

Between George Brown and John Hobbs as 'Britain's Fastest' over the standing-start quarter-mile came Ray Feltell. Riding his supercharged, 750 Triumph-engined 'Penetration', Feltell clocked 9.905 seconds and 90.86mph at Fairford in the summer of 1972 to beat Brown's long-standing 10.282 seconds/87.52mph, only to see Hobbs snatch the crown from his grasp a week later with a 9.753 second run. This is Feltell's second bike, fitted with an 820cc, Shorrock-blown, Triumph engine and two-speed Bewley transmission.

1977 Cotton LCR 250, 247cc, Rotax disc-valve single.
£2,500–3,000 COEC

The LCR 250 was built in limited numbers as a club/national racer by a small team headed by Terry Wilson.

1975 Silk 700S, 653cc, water-cooled, 2-stroke twin, Spondon chassis, double-disc front brake, drum rear.
£2,800–3,300 BKS

George Silk's first machine was a Scott-engined special entered for the 1971 Manx Grand Prix. The frame was a sturdy duplex loop affair built by Spondon Engineering. A number of the Scott-engined bikes were produced before Silk turned to building his own power unit. Laid out on similar lines to the Scott, the Silk was a water-cooled, two-stroke twin with deflector pistons and primary drive taken from the centre of the crankshaft. Production began in 1975 and continued until 1980, by which time 138 complete machines had been built. This example is a rare racing model; most Silks were roadsters.

◄ **1977 Cotton 125R,** 124cc, Rotax disc-valve single.
£2,000–2,500 COEC

The engine of this prototype had a cylinder from a water-cooled, Rotax inline engine in a one-off crankcase.

1978 MBA 'Over-the-Counter' Racer, 124cc, liquid-cooled, disc-valve, 2-stroke twin, completely restored to original specification.
£2,000–2,400 BKS

Giancarlo Morbidelli introduced his first machine in 1969, Larrarini finishing tenth that year in the 50cc Italian Grand Prix. This was quickly followed by a liquid-cooled, disc-valve, 125 twin, which was successful from the outset, winning in Czechoslovakia in 1970 and at Monza in 1971. Following the death of Morbidelli rider Gilberto Parlotti at the 1972 TT, the team took time to recover, and it was not until 1975 that it regained its winning ways, Pileri and Bianchi dominating that year's championship. This began a run that resulted in the team securing the 1976 and 1977 125 World Championships, as well as the 1977 250 World Championship with a machine that owed much to the 125 version. From 1976 onward, a production version of the 125 twin was offered as an 'over-the-counter' racer, produced by the Benelli-Armi factory in Pesaro in partnership with Morbidelli, which was reflected in the machine's MBA name.

1978 Yamaha 350TZG, 347cc, liquid-cooled, 2-stroke twin, 6-speed gearbox, cantilever rear suspension, front and rear disc brakes, aftermarket Spondon chassis.
£1,500–1,900 TGA

1979 Honda RS125, 124cc, 2-stroke, single-cylinder engine, telescopic forks, twin-shock rear suspension, front disc brake, drum rear, original apart from screen missing, in need of restoration.
£750–900 TGA

This is an early example of Honda's 'over-the-counter' single-cylinder 125 racer.

1978 Yamaha TZ350D, 347cc, liquid-cooled, 2-stroke twin, 6-speed gearbox, restored to concours condition.
£2,700–3,200 PC

This machine was raced during 1978/79 by the 1980 350cc World Champion, Jon Ekerold.

▶ **1980 Yamaha TZ350G,** 347cc, liquid-cooled, 2-stroke, twin-cylinder engine, 6-speed gearbox, Spondon frame, disc brakes, monoshock rear suspension, concours condition.
£2,000–2,500 SGR

Scooters

1953 Douglas Vespa Model ROD, 125cc, fan-cooled, 2-stroke single, 56.5 x 49.8mm bore and stroke.
£1,400–1,650 S

During the 1949 London Motorcycle Show, it was announced that the Bristol-based Douglas Company would be building Italian Vespa scooters under licence in the UK. The ROD was an early example of this Anglo-Italian venture.

1954 Vespa Model GL, 124cc, fan-cooled, 2-stroke single, dash-mounted speedometer, two carriers, restored.
£1,100–1,300 MAY

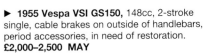

▶ **1955 Vespa VSI GS150,** 148cc, 2-stroke single, cable brakes on outside of handlebars, period accessories, in need of restoration.
£2,000–2,500 MAY

The GS150 was one of the fastest scooters of its day. Because of its rarity, this early-production GS150 is extremely valuable, even in its relatively poor condition.

◄ **1959 Vespa 100,** 98cc, 2-stroke, single-cylinder engine, pillion pad, spare wheel, unrestored.
£400–500 MAY

The Vespa 100 was not available officially in the UK, and this example was imported privately from Italy.

1956 Piatti Scooter, 125cc, 2-stroke single, 3-speed gearbox, good condition.
£500–600 AT

The Piatti was a truly international scooter, being designed by London based Italian engineer Vicenzo Piatti and built in Britain by Cyclemaster (Britax). It was also assembled in Belgium under licence.

Miller's is a price GUIDE not a price LIST

1963 Lambretta Li 150 Series 2, 148cc, fan-cooled, 2-stroke single, unrestored.
£400–500 AT

The Series 1 Li 150 had a legshield-mounted headlamp; the Series 2 had its headlamp on the handlebars, allowing the light to turn with the bars.

1964 Lambretta Li Series 3 Slimline, 124cc, 2-stroke, single-cylinder engine, in need of complete restoration.
£250–300 MAY

1964 Lambretta TV175 Series 3, 174cc, air-cooled, 2-stroke single, 62 x 58mm bore and stroke, dualseat, carrier, spare wheel.
£850–1,000 MAY

◄ 1966 Lambretta SX200, 198cc, air-cooled, 2-stroke single, 66 x 58mm bore and stroke, spare wheel, carrier, unrestored.
£2,300–2,600 IVC

The SX200 was essentially a larger-engined version of the visually identical TV175 Series 3.

1968 Vespa Sprint, 145.5cc, fan-cooled, 2-stroke single, imported to UK from Italy.
£450–500 MAY

1968 Lambretta 125 Special, 124cc, period accessories, unrestored.
£600–700 IVC

1969 Lambretta Jet 200, 198cc, air-cooled, 2-stroke, single-cylinder engine.
£650–800 MAY

The Jet 200 was made under licence by the Spanish company, Sevetta.

Cross Reference
See Colour Review

▶ **1981 Vespa T5,** 150cc, dualseat, indicators, carrier, original specification.
£650–750 MAY

1984 Vespa ETS, 125cc, fan-cooled, 2-stroke, single-cylinder engine, dualseat, integral lockable legshield compartment, original specification.
£550–650 MAY

Sidecars

1912 Bradbury Motorcycle and Mills Fulford Sidecar, 550cc, side-valve single, cast-iron piston, 2-speed epicyclic gear on engine shaft driving to rear hub clutch, period accessories including speedometer, exhaust whistle, horn, lighting and picnic basket.
£8,000–9,000 SUN

▶ **1914 Triumph Three-Speed and Wicker Sidecar,** 550cc, side-valve vertical single, flat tank, hand-change gearbox, pedal starting, belt final drive, completely restored to concours condition.
£11,500–12,500 VER

1914 Matchless Model 8B and Sidecar, 990cc, air-cooled MAG V-twin, Collier 3-speed round gearbox, coachbuilt sidecar, period accessories including curly horn, OS speedometer, acetylene lighting and Bobjon generator.
£10,600–12,000 BKS

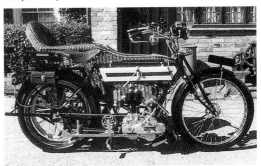

1914 BSA Model K with BSA Model 2 Sidecar, 557cc, side-valve, single-cylinder engine, caliper brakes, complete with original engine (as a spare) and several other items such as gearbox components, sidecar seat and original tonneau cover.
£7,400–8,400 BKS

This combination won many awards at vintage rallies during the 1980s and was featured in *Classic Motor Cycle* during 1983, when it had only covered about 600 miles from new.

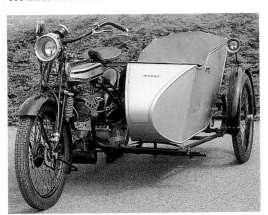

1918 Norton Big 4 and Sidecar, 633cc, side-valve single, original specification, factory-fitted lighting set.
£5,400–6,000 TEN

This motorcycle was built for military service, but was released for the civilian market.

1921 Indian Scout and Sidecar, 600cc, side-valve, 42° V-twin, 11bhp, 3-speed hand-change gearbox, single-seat sports sidecar.
£8,000–9,000 BKS

1920 Triumph Model H and Gloria Sidecar, 550cc engine, sidecar with windscreen, hood and pleated and buttoned leather upholstery.
£10,800–12,000 BKS

This restored Triumph combination broke records in 1989 when it was sold at auction for £27,500.

▶ **1925 Norton 16H and Hughes TT-Type Sidecar,** 490cc, side-valve single, 79 x 100mm bore and stroke, aluminium-bodied sidecar.
£7,750–8,750 VER

1924 New Imperial V-Twin and Sidecar, 980cc, side-valve, JAP V-twin engine, coachbuilt sidecar, period fittings including acetylene lighting, tansad pillion seat and leather side pockets.
£6,700–7,400 BKS

A New Imperial V-twin, ridden by Ginger Wood, was the first British multi-cylinder machine to achieve 100 miles within an hour.

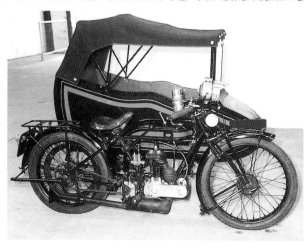

▶ **1925 Triumph Model P and Sidecar,** 500cc, side-valve single, 3-speed hand-change gearbox, all-chain drive, flat tank, coachbuilt child/adult sidecar with fixed glass windscreen and cape-cart folding hood.
£4,200–4,700 BKS

1928 BSA 5hp and Sidecar, 500cc, side-valve single, original transfers, acetylene lighting system, horn and carbide container, unrestored.
£3,900–4,300 BKS

1930 AJS R8 and Zeppelin Sidecar, 499cc, twin-port, overhead-valve single, sloping cylinder, 84 x 90mm bore and stroke, chain-driven magneto mounted behind cylinder, 'Brooklands can' exhaust.
£4,200–4,700 BKS

The R8 was replaced for the 1931 season by the S8.

Miller's is a price GUIDE not a price LIST

1939 AJS Model 2 and Watsonian Lilleshal Sidecar, 982cc, side-valve V-twin, 85.5 x 85.5mm bore and stroke, 4-speed foot-change Burman gearbox, restored 1992–96, single-seat sports sidecar.
£5,400–6,000 BKS

◄ **1944 Indian Big Chief and Sidecar,** 1200cc, ex-military model completely restored to civilian specification with valanced mudguards, chrome trim and red livery, reproduction fibreglass mudguards and sidecar body, right-hand throttle and left-hand gear-change (an option from 1930), sidecar brake, 2,000 miles covered since restoration.
£15,500–17,000 BKS

The massive 1200cc Indian V-twin engine made the Big Chief an ideal sidecar tug.

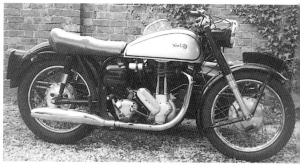

1959 Norton ES2 and Watsonian Monza Sidecar, 490cc, overhead-valve single, wideline Featherbed frame, Roadholder forks, full-width hubs, single-seat sports sidecar.
£2,900–3,250 CotC

1975 Jawa Model 559 and Type 40 Pav Trailer, 246cc, twin-port, 2-stroke single, 4-speed foot-change gearbox.
£1,200–1,400 JCZ

Both bike and trailer were built in Czechoslovakia.

1964 Greeves Trials and Sidecar, 246cc, 2-stroke single, strengthened front forks and frame.
£850–940 BKS

This special sidecar outfit was constructed with a home-made trials sidecar built from tubular steel and sheet aluminium with a Greeves wheel.

Restored values

The cost of a professional restoration will have an influence on, but no direct relation to, a motorcycle's market value. A restored motorcycle can have a market value lower than the cost of its restoration.

1993 Harley-Davidson Electra-Glide and Watsonian Monaco Sidecar, 1340cc, overhead-valve V-twin, touring accessories including panniers, top-box, 'armchair' pillion seat, extra chrome fittings, touring screen and crashbars, concours condition.
£10,000–10,500 BKS

The Electra-Glide was 20 years old when it was updated in the mid-1980s with the introduction of the much-improved Evolution engine.

Specials

1938/1940s Rudge Special, 500cc, twin-port, overhead-valve, single-cylinder engine, dualseat, rear carrier.
£1,800–2,000 TEN

This is essentially a pre-war motorcycle converted in the late 1940s to swinging-arm rear suspension.

1950s Norton Inter, 1930s overhead-camshaft Norton CSI engine, post-WWII plunger frame, telescopic forks, alloy fuel and oil tanks, racing specification.
£3,500–3,900 H&H

1950s BSA B33 Café Racer, 499cc, overhead-valve, pre-unit single, Amal Monobloc carburettor, Gold Star exhaust, central aluminium oil tank, racing tank and seat, Manx Norton flyscreen.
£2,000–2,500 MAY

This machine was built to replicate the looks of the motorcycles raced so successfully after the war by Harold Daniel and Artie Bell, until the advent of the duplex Featherbed frame, which arrived in 1950.

1954 Harley-Davidson Special, 1200cc, tuned 'panhead' motor, Drag Specialties exhaust pipes, Duo-Glide frame, drilled dual-disc front brakes, lowered suspension, 3-spoke custom wheels.
£10,500–11,600 S

c1958 Triton Special, 649cc, overhead-valve, pre-unit Triumph Thunderbird twin-cylinder engine, iron head and barrel, single carburettor, Norton 4-speed gearbox, Norton wideline Featherbed frame, twin-leading-shoe front brake conversion, touring trim with Vincent-type flat bars, Burgess silencers and steel rims.
£3,500–4,000 BLM

c1959 Triton Special, 749cc, enlarged Triumph Tiger 110 engine, 9-stud T140 top end, BSA gearbox and primary drive, BSA twin-leading-shoe front brake, Norton frame, Hagon rear shocks, Lucas chrome headlamp, steel rims, dual racing seat, alloy fuel and oil tanks.
£3,000–3,400 BLM

1960 Norton Dominator Café Racer, 597cc, Dominator 99 overhead-valve, parallel twin-cylinder engine, swept-back exhaust pipes, Dunstall megaphone silencers, twin-leading-shoe front brake, racing tank and seat, chromed oil tank and side casings, clip-ons, rearsets, alloy rims, completely restored.
£4,000–4,500 BKS

1960 BSA C15 Café Racer, 247cc, overhead-valve, unit engine, Amal Monobloc carburettor, distributor at rear of barrel, high-level exhaust, Yamaha front brake, rearsets, fork gaiters, racing seat.
£500–600 MAY

1960s Norton Domiracer Special, 597cc, various Norton twin-cylinder components, swept-back exhaust pipes, Dunstall silencers, twin-leading-shoe front brake, alloy tanks, mudguards and rims.
£2,000–2,500 MAY

◀ **1960s Triton Café Racer,** 649cc, overhead-valve, pre-unit Triumph twin-cylinder engine, splayed alloy head, twin carburettors, siamesed exhaust with single Gold Star-type silencer, 5-speed gear cluster, Norton wideline Featherbed frame, steel rims, chromed mudguards and oil tank, racing tank, dualseat.
£3,000–3,500 BLM

◄ **1959/79 BMW Special,** 800cc, overhead-valve, horizontal twin, shaft final drive.
£3,600–4,000 BMWC

Basically, this machine is a 1959 Earles-fork R60 fitted with a 1979 R80 engine, gearbox, final drive, swinging arm and rear wheel. The builder achieved a successful marriage between the two BMW model series.

1960 Triton Special, 649cc, single-carburettor, pre-unit Triumph engine, alloy head, AMC gearbox, twin-leading-shoe front brake, alloy rims, Norton Dominator wideline Featherbed frame.
£3,500–4,000 BLM

1961 Triumph Café Racer Special, 649cc, overhead-valve, pre-unit Triumph 6T twin-cylinder engine with T110 parts and later unit head and barrel, swept-back exhaust pipes and short Daytona silencers, c1969 BSA/Triumph twin-leading-shoe front brake, alloy tank, mudguards and wheel rims, stainless steel spokes, duplex frame, clip-ons, rearsets.
£2,500–2,800 HIST

1967 Triumph Flat-Track Special, 750cc, enlarged TR6C 650 overhead-valve, unit engine, gas-flowed head, twin Mikuni carburettors, racing exhaust system, Boyer ignition and oil cooler, Ceriani front forks, alloy rims, uprated shocks, alloy oil tank, San José plastic tank and seat.
£2,800–3,100 BKS

1965 BSA Lightning Café Racer, 654cc, overhead-valve unit engine, swept-back exhaust pipes, Gold Star silencers, twin-leading-shoe front brake, alloy rims, racing tank and seat, chrome chainguard, clip-ons, rearset foot controls.
£2,650–2,950 BLM

▶ **1972 Triumph Special,** 649cc, overhead-valve, unit TR6 Trophy engine, Mikuni twin carburettors, siamesed high-level exhaust, twin front discs, one-piece tank and seat base, fibreglass mudguards, square-section, aluminium swinging-arm rear suspension, Japanese front forks.
£2,600–2,900 GAZE

◄ **c1981 Triton Special,** 649cc, Triumph T120 Bonneville unit engine, twin Amal Concentric carburettors, aftermarket fairing, carrier and seat backrest.
£2,500–2,750 BKS

This Triton is unusual in that it employs a number of Japanese components, including cast alloy wheels, brake discs, calipers, sprocket carrier, front forks, mudguards, seat and electrical equipment.

1984 Moto Martin CBX Tokyo, 1047cc, Honda CBX Super Sport engine, Moto Martin chassis, Honda wheels, monoshock rear suspension.
£3,500–4,000 CBX

The French Moto Martin company built several CBX-engined specials, using their own chassis. The CBX was one of several engine types used. No more than 50 are known to exist in the UK.

1989 Lamborghini Boxer, 998cc, double-overhead-camshaft four, Ceriani adjustable forks, single-shock rear suspension, Brembo Goldline brakes, Gotti wheels, completely restored.
£8,000–8,800 BKS

During 1986, French special builder Boxer Bikes constructed a batch of 24 Kawasaki GPZ1000 RX-engined motorcycles to a design laid down by Italian supercar manufacturer Lamborghini. This particular bike is thought to be the only surviving machine with all the optional extras, including a 150bhp Yoshimura engine.

1993 Ducati Alchemy, 864cc, bevel-driven, overhead-camshaft, air-cooled V-twin engine, desmodromic valve gear, Mikuni flat-slide carburettors, short-wheelbase frame, WP inverted front forks, rising-rate rear suspension, fully-floating 280mm Brembo disc brakes.
£9,800–10,800 S

This machine is the work of Australian special builder Henry Brook, of V2 Ducati fame. It was tested by the American *Cycle World* magazine in October 1994.

Memorabilia

BADGES

Three enamelled Isle of Man TT badges, 1985, 1986 and 1989.
£8–10 each ATF

A pair of sidecar manufacturers' badges, Garrard and Swallow, 1950s.
£9–10 each ATF

An H. J. Goodman badge, 1930s, 2½in (6.5cm) wide.
£22–25 ATF

A handlebar clip badge, 'Safety First Guernsey', 1960s, 1½in (4cm) diam.
£9–10 ATF

A Butlin's Motor Cycle Club badge, 4in (10cm) high.
£30–33 PC

LOCATE THE SOURCE

The source of each illustration in Miller's can be found by checking the code letters below each caption with the Key to Illustrations on page 167.

A set of 4 BSA petrol tank badges, c1950, largest 6in (15cm) wide.
£28–32 GAZE

A set of 3 enamelled badges, Watford Joint RAC/ACU Training Scheme Instructor, Snetterton Motor Racing Club, Watford & District Motor Cycle Club, 1950–60.
£34–38 GAZE

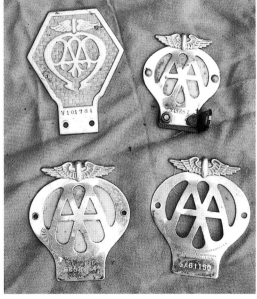

A set of 4 AA members' badges, c1935–40, largest 2½in (6.5cm) high.
£16–20 GAZE

BOOKS & BROCHURES

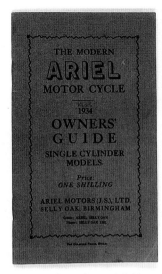

Ariel Motor Cycle Owners' Guide,
1934, 6½ x 4in (16.5 x 10cm).
£13–15 DM

BSA Motor Cycles Catalogue of
Genuine Spares, 1949 and 1951–52.
£18–22 each GAZE

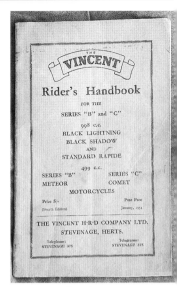

The Vincent Rider's
Handbook, 1940s.
£10–12 GAZE

The Book of the Triumph, Pitman's
Motor-Cyclists' Library, 1935–49.
£9–10 DM

An AJS Motorcycles brochure, 1936,
9½ x 7in (24 x 18cm).
£35–40 DM

Triumph Hints & Tips for
Motor Cyclists, 1915,
6 x 4½in (15 x 11.5cm).
£30–35 DM

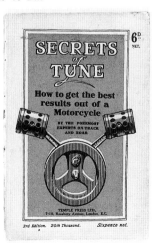

Secrets of Tune, How to get the
best results out of a Motorcycle,
3rd Edition, 1916, 7½ x 5in
(18.5 x 12.5cm).
£16–20 DM

Francis-Barnett Lightweight Models,
Hints, Instructions and Spare Parts
List, 5th edition, 1929, 7 x 5in
(18 x 12.5cm).
£12–15 DM

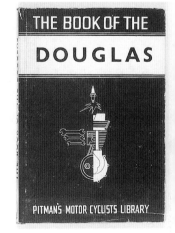

The Book of the Douglas, Pitman's
Motor-Cyclists Library, 1929–39.
£12–15 DM

◄ Spare Parts for Douglas Dragonfly
Motor Cycle, 1956, 4 x 5in
(10 x 12.5cm).
£8–10 DM

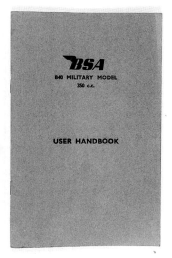

BSA B40 Military Model 350cc, User Handbook, 8 x 5½in (20.5 x 14cm).
£8–10 DM

Illustrated Spares List for Panther Motorcycles, Models 65 and 75, 1950, 10 x 6in (25.5 x 15cm).
£8–10 DM

Power and Pedal Cyclemotor & Autocycle Handbook, 1956, 7 x 5in (18 x 12.5cm).
£8–10 DM

◄ Norton Villiers Competition and Road Vehicle Engines Maintenance Manual, 1956, 8½ x 6in (21.5 x 15cm)
£8–10 DM

► Velocette Two Stroke Four Speed Model G.T.P. Spare Parts List, 1938, 8½ x 5½in (21.5 x 14cm).
£16–20 DM

Francis-Barnett Instruction Manual for Falcon, 1954, 8½ x 6in (21.5 x 15cm).
£8–10 DM

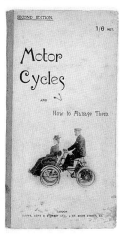

A List of Spare & Replacement Parts for the 1956 Royal Enfield 'Super Meteor', 7½ x 5in (19 x 12.5cm).
£8–10 DM

Motor Cycles and How to Manage Them, 2nd Edition, 1902, 8½ x 4½in (21.5 x 11.5cm).
£20–22 DM

► A Scott Motor Cycles brochure, 1928, 9 x 6in (23 x 15cm).
£28–35 DM

COMPONENTS

An Excelsior Talisman 250cc engine crankcase assembly and Albion gearbox, early type, c1950s.
£200–250 ETE

An Excelsior TT1 246cc, single-carburettor, 2-stroke engine, fitted with Miller generator as used on later Talisman, Mk 5 250 and 328cc engines.
£400–500 ETE

A Velocette M-series cut-away display engine, 499cc, 86 x 86mm bore and stroke, c1954.
£2,000–2,200 Velo

This display engine, built originally by Veloce for show purposes, was restored by Colin Williams during 1980–82, using internal parts donated by fellow members of the Velocette Owners' Club.

▶ A Kawasaki W1 engine and transmission assembly, late 1960s.
£160–200 GAZE

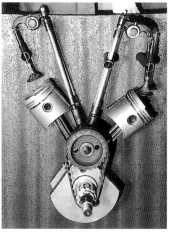

Moto Morini 3½ V-twin engine components, c1970s.
£230–260 MORI

An AJS 497cc E95 Porcupine engine, no. 5/54, original pistons, carburettors and magneto missing, accompanied by a quantity of spares including 2 new Omega pistons, various used valves, valve springs, fuel pump, inlet stubs and camshaft drive shims.
£75,000–83,000 BKS

The number of this Porcupine engine suggests that it was one of the works team's spares. The distinctive spiked cylinder head finning of the earlier E90 had disappeared by the time the E95 appeared in mid-1952; nevertheless, the Porcupine name persisted. Apart from the pressed-up crankshaft with one-piece conrods and roller big-ends, the engine remained basically much as before, although the magneto drive – one of the E90's weaknesses – was changed to a cross-shaft and chain arrangement. In this, its final incarnation, the E95 Porcupine produced a claimed 54bhp at 7,500rpm.

A Ducati 916 piston and conrod, mounted on a plinth with engraved plaque.
£2,600–2,900 S

This piston and conrod were used in the Ducati 916 ridden by Australian Troy Corser in the 1996 World Superbike Championship on 10 June, in Albacete, Spain. Corser won the championship for Ducati that year.

A 1948 Velocette KTT 348cc Mk VIII engine, gearbox and clutch assembly, engine no 950.
£7,000–8,000 BKS

The machine to which this engine, gearbox and clutch were originally fitted is believed to have been supplied to famous motorcycle racer Fergus Anderson in 1948. In the 1960s, it was installed in a special lightweight frame and ridden by John Blanchard to establish his reputation as one of the UK's foremost motorcycle racers of the day. Velocette specialist Ivan Rhodes overhauled the engine in 1985 and the gearbox in 1988, and apart from a static test, the engine has not been used since. It is fitted with a works forged piston. Although there is no proof that the gearbox was originally fitted to the Anderson machine, it is a KTT box, but not a works item.

An AMAC multiple-jet carburettor, c1920.
£50–60 GAZE

ENAMEL SIGNS

An RAC Service enamelled advertising sign, excellent condition.
£175–200 MAY

A Hutchinson enamelled advertising sign, c1950, 15 x 20in (38 x 51cm).
£100–120 EDO

A Triumph Motorcycles illuminated advertising sign, 1950, 8¼ x 14¼in (21 x 36cm).
£120–150 CRC

◄ An Ariel Motor Cycles and Cycles enamelled advertising sign, ex-Ariel factory, c1920s, 60 x 48in (152.5 x 122cm).
£100–120 BLM

► A Dunlop Cycle Tyres price card, 1915, 30 x 18in (76 x 45.5cm).
£35–40 BLM

MISCELLANEOUS

A set of 3 Everoak crash helmets.
£20–25 each MAY

A pair of Everoak crash helmets, c1940s.
£15–25 GAZE

A Lenaerts fairground ride in the form of a motorcycle, restored, working order, late 1940s.
£600–700 BKS

A Dunlop foot pump with original copper-plated finish, 16 x 6 x 4in (40.5 x 15 x 10cm).
£8–10 BLM

◄ After Pierre Falké, a lithographic print depicting a racing motorcyclist on a banked track, some surface damage and repaired tears, unmounted, laid to card, 24 x 18in (61 x 45.5cm).
£75–85 BKS

164

Key to Illustrations

Each illustration and descriptive caption is accompanied by a letter code. By referring to the following list of Auctioneers (denoted by *), Dealers (•), Clubs, Museums and Trusts (§), the source of any item may be immediately determined. Inclusion in this edition does not constitute or imply a contract or binding offer on the part of any of our contributors to supply or sell the goods illustrated, or similar articles, at the prices stated. Advertisers in this year's directory are denoted by †.

If you require a valuation, it is advisable to check whether the dealer or specialist will carry out this service and if there is a charge. Please mention Miller's when making an enquiry. A valuation by telephone is not possible. Most dealers are willing to help you with your enquiry; however, they are very busy people and consideration of the above points would be welcomed.

AMOC § AJS and Matchless Owners' Club, Northants Classic Bike Centre, 25 Victoria Street, Irthlingborough, Northamptonshire NN9 5RG Tel: 01933 652155

AOC/ AOM § Ariel Owners' Motor Cycle Club, UK Membership Secretary Paul Jameson, 23 Queen Street, Bardney, Lincolnshire LN3 5XF

AT •† Andrew Tiernan Vintage & Classic Motorcycles, Old Railway Station, Station Road, Framlingham, Nr Woodbridge, Suffolk IP13 9EE Tel: 01728 724321

ATD § Amicale du Tour du Dauphine, 82 Rue de la Chapelle, 38150 Roussillon, France

ATF • A T Fletcher (Enthusiast & Collector)

BKS *† Robert Brooks (Auctioneers) Ltd, 81 Westside, London SW4 9AY Tel: 020 7228 8000

BLM •† Bill Little Motorcycles, Oak Farm, Braydon, Swindon, Wiltshire SN5 0AG Tel: 01666 860577

BMC § British Motorcycle Owners' Club, c/o Phil Coventry, 59 Mackenzie Street, Bolton, Lancashire BL1 6QP

BMR § British Motorcycle Riders' Club, Geoff Ives, PO Box 2, Eynsham, Witney, Oxfordshire OX8 1RW

BMWC § BMW Owners' Club, Bowbury House, Kirk Langley, Derbyshire DE6 5NJ

BOC § BSA Owners' Club, Chris Taylor, PO Box 436, Peterborough, Cambridgeshire PE4 7WD Email: christaylor@natsecbsaoc. screaming.net

BRIT * British Car Auctions Ltd, Classic & Historic Automobile Division, Auction Centre, Blackbushe Airport, Blackwater, Camberley, Surrey GU17 9LG Tel: 01252 878555

BRUM • Fred Brumby Tel: 01487 842999

C * Christie, Manson & Woods Ltd, 8 King Street, St James's, London SW1Y 6QT Tel: 020 7839 9060

CARS • CARS (Classic Automobilia & Regalia Specialists), 4–4a Chapel Terrace Mews, Kemp Town, Brighton, East Sussex BN2 1HU Tel: 01273 601960

CBX § CBX Riders' Club (United Kingdom), Mel Watkins, 9 Trem Y Mynydd, Abergele, Clwyd LL22 9YY Tel: 01745 827026

CGC * Cheffins Grain & Comins, 2 Clifton Road, Cambridge CB2 4BW Tel: 01223 213343

CKC § Classic Kawasaki Club (formerly The Kawasaki Triples Club), PO Box 235, Nottingham NG8 6DT

CNI Carole Nash Insurance Consultants, Trafalgar House, 110 Manchester Road, Altrincham, Cheshire WA14 1NU Tel: 0161 9272424

COEC § Cotton Owners' Club, P Turner, Coombehayes, Sidmouth Road, Lyme Regis, Dorset DT7 3EQ

CotC •† Cotswold Classics, Ullenwood Court, Leckhampton, Nr Cheltenham, Gloucestershire GL53 9QS Tel: 01242 228622

COYS * Coys of Kensington, 2–4 Queens Gate Mews, London SW7 5QJ Tel: 020 7584 7444

CRC § Craven Collection of Classic Motorcycles, Brockfield Villa, Stockton-on-the-Forest, Yorkshire YO3 9UE Tel: 01904 488461/400493

CStC •† Cake Street Classics, Bellview, Cake Street, Laxfield, Nr Woodbridge, Suffolk IP13 8EW Tel: 01986 798504

DM • Don Mitchell & Company, 132 Saffron Road, Wigston, Leicestershire LE18 4UP Tel: 0116 277 7669

DOC * David Dockree, Cheadle Hulme Business Centre, Clemence House, Mellor Road, Cheadle Hulme, Cheshire SK7 1BD Tel: 0161 485 1258

DOT § Dot Motorcycle Club, c/o Chris Black, 115 Lincoln Avenue, Clayton, Newcastle-under-Lyne ST5 3AR

DSCM § Derbyshire and Staffordshire Classic Motorcycle Club, 51 Westwood Park, Newhall, Swadlincote, Derbyshire DE11 0R5 Tel: 01283 214542

EDO • Evariste Doublet, 30 Rue de la Gare, 19100 Lisieux, Normandie, France Tel: 00 33 (0)2 31 31 79 79

ETE § Excelsior Talisman Enthusiasts, Ginger Hall, Village Way, Little Chalfont, Buckinghamshire HP7 9PU

GAZE * Thomas Wm Gaze & Son, 10 Market Hill, Diss, Norfolk IP22 3JZ Tel: 01379 651931

GSO § Gold Star Owners' Club, Maurice Evans, 211 Station Road, Mickleover, Derby DE3 5FE

H&H *† H & H Classic Auctions Ltd, Whitegate Farm, Hatton Lane, Hatton, Warrington, Cheshire WA4 4BZ Tel: 01925 730630

HIST • Hi-Star Classics, 4 Park Lane, Herongate, Brentwood, Essex CM13 3PJ Tel: 01277 812553

ILO § International Laverda Owners' Club, c/o Alan Cudipp, 29 Claypath Road, Hetton-le-Hole, Houghton-le-Spring, Tyne & Wear DH5 0EL

IMOC § Italian Motorcycle Owners' Club (GB), John Riches, 12 Wappenham Road, Abthorpe, Towcester, Northamptonshire NN12 8QU Tel/Fax: 01327 857703

INM •† In Moto, 187 St James Road, Croydon, Surrey CR0 2BZ Tel: 020 8684 1515

IVC • The Italian Vintage Company Tel: 01673 842825

JCZ § Jawa-CZ Owners' Club, John Blackburn, 39 Bignor Road, Sheffield, Yorkshire S6 IJD

JMR • John Mossey Restorations Tel: 01763 260096

LDM § The London Douglas Motorcycle Club Ltd, Reg Holmes, 48 Standish Avenue, Stoke Lodge, Patchway, Bristol, Somerset BS34 6AG

MAY •† Mayfair Motors, PO Box 66, Lymington, Hampshire SO41 0XE Tel: 01590 644476

MOR § Morini Owners' Club, c/o Kevin Bennett, 1 Glebe Farm Cottages, Sutton Veny, Warminster, Wiltshire BA12 7AS Tel: 01985 840055

MORI § Morini Riders' Club, c/o Kevin Bennett, 1 Glebe Farm Cottages, Sutton Veny, Warminster, Wiltshire BA12 7AS Tel: 01985 840055

MSMP • Mike Smith Motoring Past, Chiltern House, Ashendon, Aylesbury, Buckinghamshire HP18 0HB Tel: 01296 651283

MVA § MV Agusta Owners Club of GB, Liz Cornish, 50 Burlingham Avenue, Evesham, Worcestershire WR11 5EF

MVT § MVT, PO Box 6, Fleet, Hampshire GU13 9PE

NLM •† North Leicester Motorcycles, Whitehill Road, Ellistown, Leicestershire LE67 1EL Tel: 01530 263381 Email: stuart@motomorini.demon.co.uk

OxM •† Oxney Motorcycles, Rolvenden, Cranbrook, Kent TN17 4QA Tel/Fax: 01797 270119

PBM § Ponthir British Motorcycle Club, 44 Emerald Street, Reath, Cardiff CF24 1QB

PC Private collection

PM •† Pollard's Motorcycles, The Garage, Clarence Street, Dinnington, Sheffield, Yorkshire S25 7NA Tel: 01909 563310

PS *† Palmer Snell, 65 Cheap Street, Sherbourne, Dorset DT9 3BA Tel: 01935 812218

REC § Rudge Enthusiasts' Club Ltd, c/o Peter Clacy (General Secretary), Bishop's Orchard, Woodway Road, Sibford Ferris, Nr Banbury, Oxfordshire OX15 5RF

RFC § Racing 50 Enthusiasts' Club, Chris Alty, 14a Kestrel Park, Ashhurst, Skelmersdale, Lancashire WN8 6TB

RM * RM Classic Cars, 825 Park Avenue West, Chatham, Ontario, Canada Tel: 00 1 519 352 4575

S *† Sotheby's, 34–35 New Bond Street, London W1A 2AA Tel: 020 7293 5000

SC • Steve's Classics, Sudbury, Suffolk Tel: 01787 377876

SGR • Steve Griffiths Racing Bikes Tel: 01788 833673

SUN § Sunbeam MCC Ltd, Ian McGill, 13 Victoria Road, Horley, Surrey RH6 9BN (A club for all makes pre-1931.)

TCTR § Tiger Cub & Terrier Register, Mike Estall, 24 Main Road, Edingale, Tamworth, Staffordshire B79 9HY Tel: 01827 383415

TDC § Tamworth & District Classic Motorcycle Club, 108 Goodwall Road, Great Barr, Birmingham B44 8RG

TDD § Tour du Dauphine en Petrolettes, 38550 St Maurice, L'Exil, France Tel: 00 33 (0)4 74 86 58 54

TEN * Tennants, 34 Montpellier Parade, Harrogate, Yorkshire HG1 2TG Tel: 01423 531661

TGA • TGA, Smithy Cottage, Liverpool Road, Blackerstaffe, Lancashire L39 0EF Tel: 01695 423621

Velo § Velocette Owners' Club, Vic Blackman, Secretary, 1 Mayfair, Tilehurst, Reading, Berkshire RG3 4RA

VER •† Verralls (Handcross) Ltd, Caffyns Row, High Street, Handcross, Haywards Heath, Sussex RH17 6BJ Tel: 01444 400678

VICO •† Toni Vico, Reg. Tre Rivi 40 12040 Monteu Rodero (CN), Piedmont, Italy Tel: 00 39 173 90121

VJMC § Vintage Japanese Motorcycle Club, PO Box 515, Dartford, Kent DA1 3RE

VMCC § Vintage Motor Cycle Club, Allen House, Wetmore Road, Burton-on-Trent, Staffordshire DE14 1TR Tel: 01283 540557

WEED • Weeden Classic Restorations, Unit 5, Atlas Court, Hermitage Ind Est, Coalville, Leicestershire LE67 3FL Tel: 01530 811118

YEST •† Yesterday's, VOF Yesterday's, Maaseikerweg 202, 6006 AD Weert, The Netherlands Tel: 00 31 (0)475 531207

Glossary

We have attempted to define some of the terms that you will come across in this book. If there are any other terms or technicalities you would like explained or you feel should be included in future editions, please let us know.

ACU – Auto Cycle Union, which controls a large part of British motorcycle sport.

Advanced ignition – Ignition timing set to cause firing before the piston reaches centre top, variation is now automatic.

Air-cooling – Most motorcycle engines rely on air-cooling, their cylinder barrels and heads being finned to dissipate heat.

Air intake – The carburettor port that admits air to mix with fuel from the float chamber.

AMCA – Amateur Motor Cycle Association, promoters of British off-road events.

APMC – The Association of Pioneer Motor Cyclists.

Auto Cycle Club – Formed in 1903, this was the original governing body of motorcycle sport. In 1907 it became the Auto Cycle Union.

Automatic inlet valve – Activated by the engine suction; forerunner of the mechanically-operated valve.

Balloon tyres – Wide-section, low-pressure tyres, fitted to tourers for comfort.

Beaded-edge tyres – Encased rubber beads in channels on wheel rim.

Belt drive – A leather or fabric belt running from the engine or gearbox to the rear wheel.

BHP – A measure of engine output: the amount of power required to lift 33,000lb to a height of 1ft in a minute equals 1bhp.

BMCRC – British Motor Cycle Racing Club, formed in 1909.

BMF – British Motorcycle Federation.

Bore/stroke ratio – The ratio of an engine's cylinder diameter to its piston stroke.

Caliper – A clamping device containing hydraulically-operated pistons that forms part of a disc brake.

Cam – Device for opening and closing a valve.

Camshaft – The mounting shaft for the cam; can be in low, high or overhead position.

Carburettor – Used to produce the air/fuel mixture required by the engine.

Chain drive – Primary form of drive from engine to gearbox and secondary gearbox to rear wheel.

Combustion chamber – Area where the fuel/air mixture is compressed and ignited, between the piston and cylinder head.

Compression ratio – The amount by which the fuel/air mixture is compressed by the piston in the combustion chamber.

Crankcase – The casing enclosing the crankshaft and its attachments.

Crankshaft – The shaft that converts the vertical motion of the piston into a rotary movement.

Cylinder – Contains the piston and is capped by the cylinder head. Upper portion forms the combustion chamber where the fuel/air mixture is compressed and burnt to provide power.

Cylinder head – Caps the top of the cylinder. In a four-stroke engine, it usually carries the valves and, in some cases, the camshaft(s).

Damper – Fitted to slow the movement in the suspension system, or as a crankshaft balance.

Displacement – The engine capacity or amount of volume displaced by the movement of the piston from bottom dead centre to top dead centre.

Distributor – A gear-driven contact that sends high-tension current to the spark plugs.

DOHC – Double overhead camshaft.

Dry sump – An engine lubrication system in which the oil is contained in a separate reservoir and pumped to and from the engine by a pair of pumps.

Earles forks – A front fork design incorporating long leading links connected by a rigid pivot behind the front wheel.

Featherbed – A Norton frame, designed by Rex and Crommie McCandless, of Belfast, used for racing machines from 1950; road machines from 1953.

FIM – Federation Internationale Motorcycliste, controls motorcycle sport world-wide.

Flat-twin – An engine featuring two horizontally-opposed cylinders.

Float – A plastic or brass box that floats upon the fuel in a float chamber and operates the needle valve controlling the fuel flow.

Flywheel – Attached to the crankshaft, this heavy wheel smooths intermittent firing impulses and helps slow running.

Friction drive – An early form of drive using discs in contact instead of chains and gears.

Gearbox – Cased trains of pinion wheels that can be moved to provide alternative ratios.

Gear ratios – Differential rates of speed between sets of pinions to provide faster or slower rotation of the rear wheel in relation to the engine speed.

GP – Grand Prix, an international race to a fixed formula.

High camshaft – Mounted high up in the engine to shorten the pushrods in an ohv arrangement.

IOE – Inlet over exhaust, a common arrangement with an overhead inlet valve and side exhaust valve.

Leaf spring – Metal blades clamped and bolted together, used in early suspension systems.

Magneto – A high-tension dynamo that produces current for the ignition spark; superseded by coil ignition.

Main bearings – Bearings in which the crankshaft runs.

Manifold – Collection of pipes supplying fuel/air mixture or removing exhaust gases.

MCC – The Motor Cycling Club, which runs sporting events; formed in 1902.

Moped – A light motorcycle of under 50cc with pedals attached.

OHC – See Overhead camshaft.

Overhead camshaft – An engine design in which the camshaft (or camshafts) is carried in the cylinder head.

OHV – See Overhead valve.

Overhead valve – A valve mounted in the cylinder head.

Pinking – A distinctive noise produced by an engine with over-advanced ignition or inferior fuel.

Piston – Moves up and down the cylinder, drawing in fuel/air mixture, compressing it, being driven down by combustion and forcing spent gases out.

Post-vintage – A motorcycle made after December 31, 1930, and before January 1, 1945.

Pressure plate – The plate against which the clutch springs react to load the friction plates.

Pushrods – Operating rods for overhead valves, working from cams below the cylinder.

Rotary valve – A valve driven from the camshaft for inlet or exhaust and usually of a disc or cylindrical shape; for either two- or four-stroke engines.

SACU – Scottish Auto Cycle Union, which controls motorcycle sport in Scotland.

SAE – Society of Automotive Engineers. Used in a system of classifying engine oils such as SAE30, l0W/50, etc.

Shock absorber – A damper, used to control vertical movement of suspension, or to cushion a drive train.

Silencer – Device fitted to the exhaust system of an engine in which the pressure of the exhaust gases is reduced to lessen noise.

Swinging arm – Rear suspension by radius arms, which carry the wheel and are attached to the frame at their forward ends.

Torque – Twisting force in a shaft; can be measured to determine at what speed an engine develops most torque.

Index to Advertisers

Bibliography

Bacon, Roy; *British Motorcycles of the 1930s*, Osprey, 1986
Bacon, Roy; *Honda The Early Classic Motorcycles*, Osprey, 1985
Bacon, Roy; *BSA Twins & Triples*, Osprey, 1980
Davis, Ivor; *It's a Triumph*, Haynes, 1980
Tragatsch, Erwin, ed; *The New Illustrated Encyclopaedia of Motorcycles*, Grange Books, 1993
Vanhouse, Norman; *BSA Competition History*, Haynes, 1986
Walker, Mick; *BMW Twins The Complete Story*, Crowood, 1998
Walker, Mick; *Laverda Twins & Triples The Complete Story*, Crowood, 1999
Walker, Mick; *Moto Guzzi Twins The Complete Story*, Crowood, 1998
Walker, Mick; *MV Agusta Fours The Complete Story*, Crowood, 2000
Walker, Mick; *Gilera The Complete Story*, Crowood, 2000
Walker, Mick; *Ducati, Fabio Taglioni and his World Beating Motorcycles*, Sutton, 2000
Walker, Mick; *British Racing Motorcycles*, Redline, 1998
Walker, Mick; *Italian Racing Motorcycles*, Redline, 1999
Walker, Mick; *German Racing Motorcycles*, Redline, 1999
Walker, Mick; *European Racing Motorcycles*, Redline, 2000
Walker, Mick; *Manx Norton*, Redline, 2000
Walker, Mick; *Hamlyn History of Motorcycling*, Hamlyn, 1997
Webster, Mike; *Classic Scooters*, Parragon, 1997
Woollett, Mick; *Norton*, Osprey, 1992

Directory of Museums

ARE Classic Bike Collection, 285 Worplesdon Road, Guildford, Surrey GU2 6XN Tel: 01483 232006
50 bikes & memorabilia. Mon & Fri 9–1pm, Tues & Thurs 9–5pm.
Atwell-Wilson Motor Museum, Downside, Stockley Lane, Calne, Wiltshire SN11 0QX
Over 60 cars & vintage, post vintage & classic motorcycles. Mon–Thur & Sun Apr–Oct 11–5pm, Nov–Mar & Good Fri 11–4pm.
Automobilia Motor Museum, The Old Mill, Terras Road, St Stephen, St Austell, Cornwall PL26 7RX Tel: 01726 823092
Around 50 vehicles 1900–66 & motorcycles. Every day except Sat in April, May & Oct 10–4pm, June–Sept every day 10–5pm.
Battlesbridge Motorcycle Museum, Muggeridge Farm, Maltings Road, Battlesbridge, Essex SS11 7RF Tel: 01268 769392
Collection of classic motorcycles & scooters. Sun 10.30–4pm.
Bradford Industrial Museum, Moorside Mills, Moorside Road, Bradford, Humberside BD2 3HP Tel: 01274 631756
General industrial museum including Jowett cars and Panther and Scott motorcycles. Tues–Fri & Bank Holidays 10–5pm
Bristol Industrial Museum, Princes Wharf, City Docks, Bristol, Gloucestershire BS1 4RN Tel: 0117 925 1470
Douglas machines, incl the only surviving V4 of 1908 and a 1972 Quasar. Tues–Sun 10–1pm & 2–5pm. Closed Thurs, Fri, Good Friday, Dec 25–27 & Jan 1.
Brooklands Museum, Brooklands Road, Weybridge, Surrey KT13 0QN Tel: 01932 857381
Motorsport and Aviation museum. About 20 motorcycles pre-WWII. Open daily summer 10–5pm, winter 10–4pm, except Mondays, Good Friday & Christmas.
Caister Castle Motor Museum, Caister-on-Sea, Nr Great Yarmouth, Norfolk Tel: 01572 787251
Cars & motorcycles from 1893. Daily mid-May–end Sept, closed Sat.
The Combe Martin Motorcycle Collection, Cross Street, Combe Martin, Ilfracombe, Devon EX34 0DH Tel: 01271 882346
100 classic & British motorcycles. Daily May–Oct 10–5pm.
Cotswold Motoring Museum & Toy Collection, Sherbourne Street, Bourton-on-the-Water, Nr Cheltenham, Gloucestershire GL54 2BY Tel: 01451 821 255
Collection of advertising signs, toys & motorcycles. Home of the Brough Superior Co and 'Brum', the small open 1920's car that has a TV series. Daily Feb–Nov 10–6pm.
Craven Collection of Classic Motorcycles, Brockfield Villa, Stockton-on-the-Forest, Yorkshire YO32 9UE Tel: 01904 488461/400493
180 vintage & post-war classic motorcycles. Open first Sun in month & Bank Hol Mon 10–4pm. Club visits & private parties.
Foulkes-Halbard of Filching, Filching Manor, Jevington Road, Wannock, Polegate, East Sussex BN26 5QA Tel: 01323 487838
100 cars 1893–1993 & 30 motorcycles incl American pre-1940's ex-Steve McQueen. Open Easter–Oct Thurs–Sun 10.30–4pm.
Geeson Bros Motorcycle Museum and Workshop, South Witham, Grantham, Lincolnshire NG33 5PH Tel: 01572 767280/768195
80 plus motorcycles restored since 1965 by the Geeson brothers. Open days throughout the year.
Grampian Transport Museum, Alford, Aberdeenshire, Scotland AB33 8AE Tel: 019755 62292
Displays and working exhibits tracing the history of travel and transport in the locality. Open April 2–Oct 31 10–5pm.
Haynes Sparkford Motor Museum, Sparkford, Yeovil, Somerset BA22 7LH Tel: 01963 440804
Haynes Publishing Co museum with collection of vintage, veteran & classic cars & motorcycles. Open daily summer 9.30–5.30pm, winter 10–4pm, except Christmas Day, Boxing Day & New Year's Day.
Historic Vehicles Collection of C. M. Booth, Falstaff Antiques, 63–67 High Street, Rolvenden, Kent TN17 4LP Tel: 01580 241234
Morgan three-wheelers, some motorbikes and memorabilia. Open Mon–Sat 10–6pm.
Lakeland Motor Museum, Holker Hall & Gardens, Cark-in-Cartmel, Grange-over-Sands, South Lakeland, Cumbria LA11 7PL
150 classic & vintage cars, tractors, cycles & engines incl about 40 motorcycles. Open end Mar–end Oct Sun–Fri 10.30–4.45pm, closed Sat.
Llangollen Motor Museum, Pentrefelin, Llangollen, Wales LL20 8EE Tel: 01978 860324
20 plus cars, 10 motorcycles, signs, tools & parts. Daily Easter–Sept 10–5pm.
London Motorcycle Museum, Ravenor Farm, 29 Oldfield Lane South, Greenford, Middlesex UB6 9LB Tel: 020 8579 1248
Collection of around 50 British motorcycles. Open weekends.

Madog Cars & Motorcycle Museum, Snowdon Street, Porthmadog, Wales LL49 9DF Tel: 01758 713618
15 cars and nearly 70 motorcycles plus memorabilia. Open May–Sept Mon–Sat 10–5pm.
Midland Motor Museum, Stanmore Hall, Stourbridge Road, Bridgnorth, Shropshire WV15 6DT Tel: 01746 762992
Collection of 60 cars and 30 motorcycles. Open daily 10.30–5pm, except Christmas Day & Boxing Day.
Sammy Miller Museum, Bashley Manor, Bashley Cross Roads, New Milton, Hampshire BH25 6TF Tel: 01425 620777
Motorcycles, artefacts & memorabilia. Open daily 10–4pm.
Moray Motor Museum, Bridge Street, Elgin, Scotland IV30 2DE Tel: 01343 544933
Cars & motorcycles plus memorabilia & diecast models. Daily Easter–Oct 11–5pm.
Mouldsworth Motor Museum, Smithy Lane, Mouldsworth, Chester CH3 8AR Tel: 01928 731781
Over 60 cars, motorcycles & early bicycles in 1937 Art Deco building. Open Sun Mar–end Nov 12–5pm, incl all bank holidays & weekends, also Weds in July & Aug 1–5pm.
Murray's Motorcycle Museum, Bungalow Corner, Mountain Road, Snaefell, Isle of Man Tel: 01624 861719
140 machines, including Mike Hailwood's 250cc Mondial & Honda 125cc. Open May–Sept 10–5pm.
Museum of British Road Transport, St Agnes Lane, Hales Street, Coventry, Warwickshire CV1 1PN Tel: 024 7683 2425
Around 100 motorcycles. Daily 10–5pm, except Dec 24–26.
Museum of Transport, Kelvin Hall, 1 Bunhouse Road, Glasgow, Scotland G3 8DP Tel: 0141 357 2656/2720
A museum devoted to the history of transport on the land. Open daily 10–5pm, Sun 11–5pm, except Dec 25 & Jan 1.
Myreton Motor Museum, Aberlady, Longniddry, East Lothian, Scotland EH32 0PZ Tel: 01875 870288
Cars, motorcycles, commercials & WWII military vehicles. Daily 10am except Christmas Day. Parties & coaches welcome.
National Motor Museum, Brockenhurst, Beaulieu, Hampshire SO42 7ZN Tel: 01590 612123/612345
Over 200 cars, 60 motorcycles & memorabilia. Open daily from 10am, closed Dec 25.
National Motorcycle Museum, Coventry Road, Bickenhill, Solihull, West Midlands B92 0EJ Tel: 01675 443311
Over 650 restored motorcycles. Open daily 10–6pm, except Christmas Day & Boxing Day.
National Museum of Scotland, The Granton Centre, 242 West Granton Rd, Edinburgh, Scotland EH1 1JF Tel: 0131 551 4106
Small display of engines & complete machines includes the world's first four-cylinder motorcycle, an 1895 Holden. Tours available, book in advance.
Newburn Hall Motor Museum, 35 Townfield Gardens, Newburn, Tyne & Wear NE15 8PY Tel: 0191 264 2977
About 50 cars & 10 motorcycles. Daily 10–6pm, except Mon.
Norfolk Motorcycle Museum, Station Approach, North Walsham, Norfolk NR28 0DS Tel: 01692 406266
100 motorcycles 1920–60s. Daily 10–4.30pm, closed Sun in winter.
Ramsgate Motor Museum, West Cliff Hall, Ramsgate, Kent CT11 9JX Tel: 01843 581948
Open April–Nov 10.30–5.30pm, winter Sun 10–5pm.
Shuttleworth Collection, Old Warden Aerodrome, Nr Biggleswade, Bedfordshire SG18 9EP Tel: 01767 627288
Collection of flying pre-1940 aircraft & veteran & vintage vehicles, incl 15 motorcycles. Daily 10–3pm, 4pm Mar–Oct.
Stanford Hall Motorcycle Museum, Stanford Hall, Lutterworth, Leicestershire LE17 6DH Tel: 01788 860250 Fax: 01788 860870 Email: stanford.hall@virginnet.co.uk
Collection of racing and vintage motorcycles. Open Sat, Sun, Bank Holiday Mon & following Tues, Easter–Sept 2.30–5.30pm.
Stondon Museum, Station Road, Lower Stondon, Henlow, Bedfordshire SG16 6JN Tel: 01462 850339
Over 320 transport exhibits including Bentleys & 30-plus motorcycles. Open daily 10–5pm.
Ulster Folk & Transport Museum, Cultra, Holywood, Co Down, Northern Ireland BT18 0EU Tel: 028 90 428 428
Includes 70–100 motorcycles. Open daily 10.30–5/6pm, Sun 12–6pm; closed Christmas.
Western Lakes Motor Museum, The Maltings, Brewery Lane, Cockermouth, Cumbria Tel: 01900 824448
Some 45 cars and 17 motorcycles from Vintage to Formula 3. Open daily Mar–Oct 10–5pm. Closed Jan; other months weekends only.
Whitewebbs Museum of Transport, Whitewebbs Road, Enfield, Middlesex EN2 9HW Tel: 020 8367 1898
Collection of commercial vehicles, cars and 20–30 motorcycles. Ring for opening times.

Directory of Motorcycle Clubs

If you wish to be included in next year's directory, or if you have a change of address or telephone number, please inform us by 27 April 2001.

ABC Owners' Club, D A Hales, The Hedgerows, Sutton St Nicholas, Hereford HR1 3BU Tel: 01432 880726

Aircooled RD Club, Susan Gregory, Membership Secretary, 6 Baldwin Road, Burnage, Greater Manchester M19 1LY Tel: 0161 286 7539

AJS & Matchless Owners' Club, Northants Classic Bike Centre, 25 Victoria Street, Irthlingborough, Northamptonshire NN9 5RG Tel: 01933 652155

AMC Owners' Club, c/o Terry Corley, 12 Chilworth Gardens, Sutton, Surrey SM1 3SP

Androd Classics, 70 Broadway, Frome, Somerset BA11 3HE Tel: 01373 471087

Ariel Owners' Motor Cycle Club, UK Membership Secretary, Paul Jameson, 23 Queen Street, Bardney, Lincolnshire LN3 5XF

Ariel Owners' Motor Cycle Club, Swindon Branch, Paul Hull, Branch Secretary, Turnpike Cottage, Marlborough Road, Wootton Bassett, Wiltshire SN4 7SA

Association of Pioneer Motorcyclists, Mrs J MacBeath, Secretary, 'Heatherbank', May Close, Headley, Nr Bordon, Hampshire GU35 8LR

Bantam Enthusiasts' Club, c/o Vic Salmon, 16 Oakhurst Close, Walderslade, Chatham, Kent ME5 9AN

Benelli Motobi Riders' Club, Steve Peace, 43 Sherrington Road, Ipswich, Suffolk IP1 4HT Tel: 01473 461712

Best Feet Forward MCC, Paul Morris, Membership Secretary, 43 Finedon Road, Irthlingborough, Northamptonshire NN9 5TY

BMW Club, c/o Mike Cox, 22 Combermere, Thornbury, Bristol, Gloucestershire BS35 2ET Tel/Fax: 01454 415358

BMW Owners' Club, Bowbury House, Kirk Langley, Derbyshire DE6 5NJ

Bristol & District Sidecar Club, 158 Fairlyn Drive, Kingswood, Bristol, Gloucestershire BS15 4PZ

Bristol Genesis Motorcycle Club, Burrington, 1a Bampton Close, Headley Park, Bristol, Gloucestershire BS13 7QZ Tel: 0117 978 2584

British Motor Bike Owners' Club, c/o Ray Peacock, Crown Inn, Shelfanger, Diss, Norfolk IP22 2DL

British Motorcycle Association, Pete Reed, AMCA, 28 Mill Park, Hawks Green Lane, Cannock, Staffordshire WS11 2XT

British Motorcycle Club of Guernsey, c/o Ron Le Cras, East View, Village De Putron, St Peter Port, Guernsey, Channel Islands GY1

British Motorcycle Owners' Club, c/o Phil Coventry, 59 Mackenzie Street, Bolton, Lancashire BL1 6QP

British Motorcycle Riders' Club, Geoff Ives, PO Box 2, Eynsham, Witney, Oxfordshire OX8 1RW

British Motorcyclists' Federation, Jack Wiley House, 129 Seaforth Avenue, Motspur Park, New Malden, Surrey KT3 6JU

British Two-Stroke Club, Mrs Lynda Tanner, Membership Secretary, 259 Harlestone Road, Duston, Northampton NN5 6DD Tel: 01604 581516

BSA Owners' Club, Chris Taylor, PO Box 436, Peterborough, Cambs PE4 7WD Email: christaylor@natsecbsaoc.screaming.net

CBX Riders' Club (United Kingdom), Mel Watkins, 9 Trem Y Mynydd, Abergele, Clwyd LL22 9YY Tel: 01745 827026

Christian Motorcyclists' Association, PO Box 113, Wokingham, Berkshire RG11 5UB Tel: 0870 606 3610 Email: cma-admin@bike.org.uk Website: www.bike.org.uk/cma/

Classic Kawasaki Club, (Formerly The Kawasaki Triples Club), PO Box 235, Nottingham NG8 6DT

Classic Racing Motorcycle Club Ltd, Ron Key, 6 Cladgate Grove, Wombourne, Wolverhampton, West Midlands WV5 8JS

Cossack Owners' Club, Alan Mottram, Membership Sec, 19 The Villas, West End, Stoke on Trent, Staffordshire ST4 5AQ

Cotton Owners' Club, P Turner, Coombehayes, Sidmouth Road, Lyme Regis, Dorset DT7 3EQ

Derbyshire and Staffordshire Classic Motorcycle Club, 51 Westwood Park, Newhall, Swadlincote, Derbyshire DE11 0R5 Tel: 01283 214542

Dot Motorcycle Club, c/o Chris Black, 115 Lincoln Avenue, Clayton, Newcastle-under-Lyne ST5 3AR

Edge & District Vintage Motorcycle Club, 10 Long Lane, Larkton, Malpas, Cheshire SY14 8LP

Exeter British Motorcycle Club, c/o Bill Jones, 7 Parkens Cross Lane, Pinhoe, Exeter, Devon EX1 3TA

Exeter Classic Motorcycle Club, c/o Martin Hatcher, 11 Newcombe Street, Heavitree, Exeter, Devon EX1 2TG

Federation of Sidecars, Jeff Reynard, 5 Ethel Street, Beechcliffe, Keighley, Yorkshire BD20 6AN

Fellowship of Christian Motorcyclists, Phil Crow, 6 St Anne's Close, Formby, Liverpool, Merseyside L37 7AX

FJ Owners' Club, Lee & Mick Beck, Membership Secretary, 1 Glen Crescent, Stamford, Lincolnshire PE9 1SW

Forgotten Racing Club, Mrs Chris Pinches, 73 High Street, Morton, Bourne, Lincolnshire PE10 0NR Tel: 01778 570535

Francis Barnett Owners' Club, Sue Dorling, Club Secretary, Clouds Hill, 5 Blacklands Road, Upper Bucklebury, Nr Reading, Berkshire RG7 6QP Tel: 01635 864256

Gilera Network, Pete Fisher, 4 Orton Grove, Penn, Wolverhampton WV4 4JN Tel: 01902 337626

Gold Star Owners' Club, Maurice Evans, 211 Station Road, Mickleover, Derby DE3 5FE

Goldwing Owners' Club, 82 Farley Close, Little Stoke, Bristol, Gloucestershire BS12 6HG

Greeves Owners' Club, c/o Dave McGregor, 4 Longshaw Close, North Wingfield, Chesterfield, Derbyshire S42 5QR

Greeves Riders' Association, Dave & Brenda McGregor, 4 Longshaw Close, North Wingfield, Chesterfield, Derbyshire S42 5QR Tel: 01246 853846

Harley-Davidson Riders' Club of Great Britain, SAE to Membership Secretary, PO Box 62, Newton Abbott, Devon TQ12 2QE

Harley-Davidson UK, The Bell Tower, High Street, Brackley, Northamptonshire NN13 7DT Tel: 01280 700101 Websites: www.harley-davidson.co.uk www.harley-davidson.com

Harley Owners' Group, HOG UK, The Bell Tower, High St, Brackley, Northamptonshire NN13 7DT Tel: 01280 700101

Hedingham Sidecar Owners' Club, John Dean, Membership Secretary, Birchendale Farm, Fole Lane, Stoke-on-Trent, Staffordshire ST10 4HL Tel: 01889 507389

Hesketh Owners' Club, Peter White, 1 Northfield Road, Soham, Cambridgeshire CB7 5UE Tel: 01353 720550

Honda Monkey Club, 28 Newgate Road, off Red Lane, Coventry, Warwickshire CV6 5ES Tel: 024 7666 5141

Honda Owners' Club (GB), Membership Sec, 61 Vicarage Road, Ware, Hertfordshire SG12 7BE Tel: 01932 787111

Indian Motorcycle Club, c/o John Chatterton, Membership Secretary, 183 Buxton Road, Newtown, Disley, Stockport, Cheshire SK12 2RA Tel: 01663 747106

International Laverda Owners' Club, c/o Alan Cudipp, 29 Claypath Road, Hetton-le-Hole, Houghton-le-Spring, Tyne & Wear DH5 0EL

International Motorcyclists' Tour Club, James Clegg, 238 Methane Road, Netherton, Huddersfield, Yorkshire HD4 7HL Tel: 01484 664868

Italian Motorcycle Owners' Club (GB), John Riches, 12 Wappenham Road, Abthorpe, Towcester, Northamptonshire NN12 8QU Tel/Fax: 01327 857703

Jawa-CZ Owners' Club, John Blackburn, 39 Bignor Road, Sheffield, Yorkshire S6 IJD

Kawasaki GT Club, D Shucksmith, Club Secretary, Flat K, Lichfield Court, Lichfield Road, Walsall, West Midlands WS4 2DX Tel: 01922 37441

Kawasaki Riders' Club, Gemma Court, 1 Concord House, Kirmington, Humberside DN39 6YP

The Kettle Club, Shaun Chandler, 66 Provene Gardens, Waltham Chase, Southampton, Hampshire SO32 2LE

Kickstart Club Torbay, c/o Eddie Hine, 12 Vale Road, Kingskerswell, Newton Abbot, Devon TQ12 5AE

Laverda Owners' Club, c/o Ray Sheepwash, 8 Maple Close, Swanley, Kent BR8 7YN

LE Velo Club Ltd, P Walker, Grantley House, Warwicks Bench, Guildford, Surrey GU1 3SZ

Leader and Arrow Club, Stan Davies, 11 Hollins Lane, Tilstock, Whitchurch SY13 3NT

Leominster Classic MCC, Ron Moore, The Yew Tree, Gorsty, Pembridge, Herefordshire HR6 9JF

The London Douglas Motorcycle Club Ltd, Reg Holmes, 48 Standish Avenue, Stoke Lodge, Patchway, Bristol, Somerset BS34 6AG

London Sidecar Club, 107 Silverweed Road, Walderslade, Chatham, Kent ME5 0RF Tel: 01634 864298

Maico Owners' Club, c/o Phil Hingston, 'No Elms', Goosey, Faringdon, Oxfordshire SN7 8PA Tel: 01367 710408

Marston Sunbeam Register, Ray Jones, 37 Sandhurst Drive, Penn, Wolverhampton, West Midlands WV4 5RJ

Morini Owners' Club, c/o Kevin Bennett, 1 Glebe Farm Cottages, Sutton Veny, Warminster, Wiltshire BA12 7AS Tel: 01985 840055

Morini Riders' Club, c/o Kevin Bennett, 1 Glebe Farm Cottages, Sutton Veny, Warminster, Wiltshire BA12 7AS Tel: 01985 840055

Moto Guzzi Club GB, Polly Foyle, Membership Secretary, 43 Poplar Avenue, Bedworth, Warwickshire CV12 9EW

MV Agusta Owners' Club of GB, Liz Cornish, 50 Burlingham Avenue, Evesham, Worcestershire WR11 5EF

MVT, PO Box 6, Fleet, Hampshire GU13 9PE

National Association of Supertwins, Sue Beneke, 10A Queens Road, Evesham, Worcestershire

National Autocycle & Cyclemotor Club, Rob Harknett, 1 Parkfields, Roydon, Harlow, Essex CM19 5JA

National Sprint Association, Judith Sykes, Secretary, 10 Compton Street, Clifton, York YO3 6LE

National Trailers Owners' Club (NaTo), 47c Uplands Avenue, Rowley, Regis Warley, West Midlands B65 9PU

New Imperial Owners' Association, Mrs J E Jarvis, Lyndhurst House, Victoria Road, Hayling Island, Hampshire PO11 0LU Tel: 023 9246 9098

North Devon British Motorcycle Owners' Club, D E Davies, 47 Old Town, Bideford, Devon EX39 3BH Tel: 01237 472237

Norton Owners' Club, Colin Coleman, 110 Skegby Road, Annesley Woodhouse, Nottinghamshire NG17 9FF

Norton Owners' Club, c/o Philip Hill, Secretary, 11 Hammond Close, Thatcham, Newbury, Berkshire RG19 4FF

Norton Rotary Enthusiasts' Club, Alan Jones, 112 Fairfield Crescent, Newhall, Swadlingcote DE11 0TB

Panther Owners' Club, Graham & Julie Dibbins, Oakdene, 22 Oak Street, Netherton, Dudley, West Midlands DY2 9LJ

Racing 50 Enthusiasts' Club, Chris Alty, 14a Kestrel Park, Ashhurst, Skelmersdale, Lancashire WN8 6TB

Raleigh Safety Seven & Early Reliant Owners' Club incorporating Historic Raleigh Motorcycle Club, Mick Sleap, 17 Courtland Avenue, Chingford, London E4 6DU Tel: 020 8524 6310

Rolls Royce Vintage & Classic Motorcycle Club, Ken Birch, 111 Havenbaulk Lane, Littleover, Derby DE23 7AD

Rotary Owners' Club, c/o David Cameron, Dunbar, Ingatestone Road, Highwood, Chelmsford, Essex CM1 3QU

Royal Automobile Club, PO Box 700, Bristol, Gloucestershire BS99 1RB Tel: 01454 208000

Royal Enfield Owners' Club, Sylvia & Mick Seager, 30/32 Causeway, Burgh-Le-Marsh, Skegness, Lincolnshire PE24 5LT

Rudge Enthusiasts' Club Ltd, c/o Peter Clacy, General Secretary, Bishop's Orchard, Woodway Road, Sibford Ferris, Nr Banbury, Oxfordshire OX15 5RF

Rudge Enthusiasts' Club Ltd, Bloomsbury, 13 Lade Fort Crescent, Lydd-on-Sea, Romney Marsh, Kent TN29 9YG Tel: 01797 367029 Fax: 01797 361565 Website: www.rudge.ndirect.co.uk

Scott Owners' Club, Brian Marshall, Press Officer, Walnut Cottage, Abbey Lane, Aslockton, Nottingham NG13 9AE Tel/Fax: 01949 851027

Shrivenham Motorcycle Club, 12–14 Townsend Road, Shrivenham, Swindon, Wiltshire SN6 8AS

Sidecar Register, c/o John Proctor, 112 Briarlyn Road, Birchencliffe, Huddersfield, Yorkshire HD3 3NW

South Wales Sunbeam MCC, Kate Baxter, 17 Heol-Glynog Beddau, Pontypridd, South Wales

Street Specials Motorcycle Club inc Rickman O/C, Harris O/C & Featherbed O/C, c/o Dominic Dawson, 12 St Mark's Close, Gosport, Hampshire PO12 2DB Tel: 023 9250 1321

Sunbeam MCC Ltd, Ian McGill, 13 Victoria Road, Horley, Surrey RH6 9BN A club for all makes pre-1931.

Sunbeam Owners' Club, Stewart Engineering, Church Terrace, Harbury, Leamington Spa, Warwickshire CV33 9HL

Sunbeam Owners' Fellowship, c/o Stewart Engineering, Church Terrace, Harbury, Leamington Spa, Warwickshire CV33 9HL

Suzuki Owners' Club, PO Box 7, Egremont, Cumbria CA22 2GE

Tamworth & District Classic Motorcycle Club, 108 Goodwall Road, Great Barr, Birmingham B44 8RG

Tiger Cub & Terrier Register, Mike Estall, 24 Main Road, Edingale, Tamworth, Staffordshire B79 9HY Tel: 01827 383415

Tour du Dauphine en Petrolettes, 38550 St Maurice L'Exil, France Tel: 04 74 86 58 54

Trail Riders' Fellowship, Tony Stuart, 'Cambrea', Trebetherick, Wadebridge, Cornwall PL27 6SG Tel: 01208 862960

Trident & Rocket 3 Owners' Club, John Atkins, Club Secretary, 47 Underhill Road, Benfleet, Essex SS7 1EP

Triumph Motorcycle Club, 6 Hortham Lane, Almondsbury, Bristol, Gloucestershire BS12 4JH

Triumph Owners' MCC, Mrs M M Mellish, General Secretary, 4 Douglas Avenue, Harold Wood, Romford, Essex RM3 0UT

Triumph Triples Club, H J Allen, 50 Sylmond Gardens, Rushden, Northamptonshire NN10 9EJ

Velocette Owners' Club, Vic Blackman, Secretary, 1 Mayfair, Tilehurst, Reading, Berkshire RG3 4RA

Veteran Grass Track Riders' Association (VGTRA), Tel: 01622 204745

Veteran Vespa Club, Ashley Lenton, 3 Vincent Road, Croydon, Surrey CR0 6ED Tel: 020 8656 4953

Vincent-HRD Owners' Club, c/o John Wilding, Little Wildings, Fairhazel, Piltdown, Uckfield, East Sussex TN22 3XB Tel: 01825 763529

Vintage Japanese Motorcycle Club, PO Box 515, Dartford, Kent DA1 3RE

Vintage Motor Cycle Club, Allen House, Wetmore Road, Burton-on-Trent, Staffordshire DE14 1TR Tel: 01283 540557

Vintage Motor Scooter Club, c/o Ian Harrop, 11 Ivanhoe Avenue, Lowton St Lukes, Nr Warrington, Cheshire WA3 2HX

Virago Owners' Club, John Bryning, President, River Green House, Great Sampford, Saffron Walden, Essex CB10 2RS Tel: 01799 586578

Vmax Club, H Doyle, 87 Honiton Road, Wyken, Coventry, Warwickshire CV2 3EF Tel: 024 7644 2054

Yamaha Riders' Club, Alan Cheney, 11 Lodden Road, Farnborough, Hampshire GU14 9NR

ZI Owners' Club, c/o Jerry Humpage, 90 Delves Crescent, Walsall, West Midlands WS5 4LT

Zundapp Bella Enthusiasts' Club, Bill Dorling, Chairman, 5 Blacklands Road, Upper Bucklebury, Reading, Berkshire RG7 6QP

Index

Italic page numbers denote colour pages; **bold** numbers refer to information and pointer boxes